CHASING THE WIND UNDER THE SUN

By,

Victor Dias DeSousa

CHASING THE WIND UNDER THE SUN

Copyright © 2020 Victor Dias DeSousa

All rights reserved.

ISBN-13: 9798682757190

Special thanks to

V. Stevenson

M. DeSousa

T. Kallish

M. Castro

Graphic Layout & Design by, Vania Stevenson

For Paulo my immediate brother before me, who so prematurely departed from us. An aching soul with a burning desire to provide comfort at any cost to all who depended on him. Either of joy or profound sadness I remember the tears being disproportionately more than the smiles. Those smiles I am keeping in the very deep treasure trove of my fondest memories. I miss him every day.

To my oldest bother Herculano who bears our father's name. More than I ever desired we remain still separated by thousands of miles, yet never really away from each other. Lano may never have realized the comfort I desperately needed and felt every time the large doors at the arrival gate of a new airport opened me to a new reality, that I could be assured he would be there smiling and waving, welcoming me with open arms, transforming the new step in a new alien world, not so unknown and much less intimidating. By simply being there in every crucial moment of my life he was not only my hero at time, but always my one and only adult reference and my role model. In every single one of those moments he became my hope personified.

To the four mothers in my life.

To Ilda, my birth mother, the good soil where my roots took hold who always taught me not to stay silent when witnessing injustices being committed and to always have an ample supply of compassion and mercy so that when your time comes, you die standing like the trees.

To Tina the mother of my daughters, my shield against adversity who like a metronome makes sure my pace is in tempo, while being my anchor holding me firm afloat when facing the stormy seas of life.

To Tania and Vania my two daughters who by becoming mothers themselves complete the full circle of life and who keep me centered, offer me plenty of reflection and provide me with a purposeful direction to successfully navigate the complex map of life.

"Life isn't just about taking in oxygen and giving out carbon dioxide"

~Malala Yousafzai

INTRODUCTION

Sitting here with my feet on the rail of the balcony, pressed against this mountain that starts it's ascent about 10 yards from where I am, I can hear all kinds of birds singing, a faceoff acapella between yellow finches, cardinals and even woodpeckers. I hear the frogs croaking, maybe celebrating this warmer day of what has been an unusually cold and rainy April, by a living stream that runs down the mountain and passes right by where I am. I can hear the fresh crystalline waters running in honor of a planet that is breathing better than the humans in these Covid quarantine times. I can hear the cicadas in their incessant dialogue. The dense forest still semi naked, gives me serenity by a gentle whispering breeze bringing me down to a semi hypnotic gaze, in a moment of respite and self-awareness. Here I am, not able to close my eyes but focusing on every single detail I can catch. It feels like I have a 20/20 vision again and an unexpected aroma invades an almost forgotten sense of smell......where have I been ever transported by these sounds, this aroma , this cool breeze in the air ? Why does it feel so familiar and why do I feel this strange sentiment of yearning, this uncontrollable impulse to allow tears to roll down my face in an amalgam of undefined joy and welcomed sadness? Where is my mind? Where is my spirit? I can't close my eyes for I am afraid that if I do, this magic journey of my soul goes away. Need to keep them open so I can keep dreaming. I want this breathing to never stop. I want to share this voyage with my loved ones, kiss my wife, hold her tight in my arms and let my smile and my tears tell the story. Where is this ecstasy coming from? I know this smell, I have felt this breeze and heard these sounds before......then it hit me....Aaahhhh...Africa. I found my piece of Africa at the base of a mountain, 10 yards away from me in Northwest New Jersey.

1

I grew up listening to stories. Until I was almost 18 years old I had not laid eyes on a television. There was no such thing in Mozambique. And now over 40 years later I reflect upon the times fantasizing about having one, what I may have missed , what details I may have ignored that only not having one, would allow me to witness.

So my upbringing was supported by stories, either told by my mother, the indigenous people or the radio. One of my fondest memories of joy in my childhood was the first time I laid my hands on a small transistor radio I could put under my pillow at night listening to "The voice of the jungle" until I fell asleep. When my father died in a horrific car accident on a trip back from South Africa I used to climb into my mother's bed at night. I had heard her cry in hiding so many times after that, I wanted to comfort her but most certainly I needed her comfort and her warmth at night. I still remember her smile and even a look of gratitude when I did not let her sleep alone during those nights, and it was in a couple of those nights that together we heard on the radio the live broadcast of the famous "Thrilla in Manila" between Cassius Clay and Joe Frazier.

And the famous declaration "small step for a man, giant step for mankind" professed by Neil Armstrong. Those radio anchors or DJ's had a talent worthy of the biggest rewards from gods.

2

Our house was a building divided in four quadrilaterals as it would be known today. Big divisions, surrounded by a driveway as long as a football field, garage and backyard. A front yard protected by a 4 foot cement wall was an added bonus to tenants in the ground floor which was our case. Connecting our next door neighbors, both driveways 'ours on the left theirs on the right was a large fully cemented extra area intended for the servants' quarters.

Our second next door neighbor was a basketball coach who had played in one of the top teams of the city, so that area initially intended to provide the servants with some dignified privacy became our basketball court with two boards installed by those whose privacy we were usurping. Their quarters were unsophisticated, two edifications made with cement, composed of four independent rooms, without windows, where they were allowed to sleep if they wished and a bathroom across a small passageway.

Sebastian, our faithful "Full servant" called a "mainato" name given to an African house worker, who performs all the chores as a house maid from cooking to ironing and cleaning, very rarely slept in. I realized as I was growing older and more conscientious about our condition as a white African colonialist that he walked home to his hut and his wives after work every day. Sebastian did not have a day off but I believe in our house he was "allowed" not to work on Sunday, a very unusual grace given to servants. I think of Sebastian still today with a deep sense of reverence and my penalty for this privilege, I was born into, is the fact I never had the opportunity to apologize to him, for his diligence in ironing and washing my clothes, cooking my meals and having to look at me, a child yet not able to aim properly at the center of the toilet bowl, as his "young master". That bowl he had to clean often by the way. Sebastian lived close to 10 kilometers away from where he worked, which was common. The beautiful city of LM, Pearl of the Indian Ocean, as it was known did not allow it's aesthetics to be bothered by the site of a different kind of civilization in the suburbs.

10 kilometers he walked everyday back to his hut after or around 9 o'clock after his work was considered done, and was allowed to leave, and 10 miles back to be at work again no later than 7 in the morning. When my awakening started happening,

I very gradually became aware of some things that did not make sense to me such as "why did Sebastian do this walk so many times barefooted?"

3

That day in October 1969, I could sense the tension in the air. My mother felt uneasy, sitting for brief moments in the living room, getting up looking for something in the kitchen, going back to the living room only to get up, go out to the front veranda and sit staring at nothing, just facing the public park that rested right across the street. I loved to sit there from time to time. There was some activity on these blooming acacia trees laced sidewalks and the possibility of always going across and playing in the park at will, but mostly I sat there observing the ritual of the lizards that were so prevalent in our area. It would take a chameleon a good half hour, to get past the six foot mark, changing colors according to what they faced on the way while with the precision of a laser projecting their tongues out and capturing their meals. Most fascinating to me was to watch the gala-galas, a reasonably large lizard, larger than most displaying their either reddish or blue colored heads looking for food. They can grow a bit longer than a foot and are known to eat other smaller lizards, spiders and even eggs of other reptiles and birds. There are all kinds of lizards in that part of the world. I was uncomfortable with my mother behaving like a lioness in the bush when she senses danger and her cubs are at risk. My mother had a unique capability of suffering and worrying in silence, but that day her facial expressions and body language told a different story. I decided to grab an old Slazenger tennis racket my oldest brother had given me, before leaving to study in Europe, and with a couple of tennis balls practice my volley against a wall that divided our property from our neighbor's.

Time passed inexorably and I could not explain why this was an unwelcome event, then it dawned on me that my father and my older brother were on the way home from a trip to South Africa.

They were being driven by a close friend and next door neighbor from our building. I was playing a good 50 yards away from the house but can still hear the chilling scream coming from inside and my mother's voice shouting for me "Vitooo"....."Vitooo" - that's what the family called me. I ran inside only to see my mother running towards me in complete desperation crying "Dad died ...he died!!!" while falling on her knees and squeezing me in her arms. I was 9 years old. The house started getting filled with people, many of whom I did not know, and I was crying in the corner of our dining room not sure why. In a blur what I remember the most, is my grown up cousin finding me, putting his finger in my face and telling me "I want you to be strong, you hear me?" I don't remember being very close to my father, my memories of him were blurry but the pain my mother was feeling was too contagious. And what about my brother? Did he die too?

He was in the ICU of the only hospital in the city and still did not know what had happened to my father. They were really close.

My father apparently was very popular. I only came in contact with the details of the accident through a newspaper article that my family had hidden from me all my life. It was not until many years later that I laid my eyes on a local newspaper article that reported the accident.

Reading it, I now understand why I was spared the details. I did not go to my father's funeral, but watched the procession from the 11th floor apartment of a good friend of the family. She had a rosary in her hands passing the beads from finger to finger, tears in her eyes and her mouth moving in silence. I believed she was praying, but she was able to count the number of cars following the hearse, 70 she said. The newspaper article confirmed how much my father was liked. Mother had another test to face however. Within days and with a couple of good old friends they had to tell my brother what had happened as it was strongly recommended not to tell him while recovering in the hospital. All that time my brother believed our father was waiting for him at home.

These were long, hard sad days. My mother was trying to find a new compass in life. I knew how much they loved and depended on each other's love. He had been married before and became a widower with two teenage children. My mother marrying him became a step mother of these two new human beings and the anchor he needed in a time of uncertainty.

I cannot remember a time in which I saw them fighting. All the memories are loaded with smiles and hope. The accident could have been attributed to our friend, the driver of the car, going at extreme high speed on a road typical of those of Africa. Not very wide and sinuous at times. From my brother's late recollection my father had asked him to slow down but he wanted to get home sooner than later, and that Citroen would get them there. This trip was planned so my brother could see a renowned back specialist, so for the rest of his life Paulo carried with him an unshakeable sense of guilt.

The speed was too much for John to avoid a tractor trailer, backing up from a side property, when he realized another car was coming in the opposite direction. John only had a fractured leg and needed a knee replacement, Paulo was in a coma and the ICU for quite some time and my father lost his life.

What I remember, sometime after, is seeing one uncle of mine coming inside our house yelling at his sister, insulting her and calling her a thief of her children's future.

He had initiated the necessary steps to sue and collect a hefty sum of money from John, but my mother refused. There was already enough pain, she said, and John's was not lesser than hers for sure. She refused to share her own suffering by inflicting even a deeper wound on the man responsible for the loss of her soul mate. I remember after that episode and my uncle storming out of the house - he did not talk to her for a significant while after that - John with his wife and kids ringing the front door bell. He could not face me and my brother. All he could do was with an uncontrollable sob beg my mother for forgiveness. They had been the closest of friends for years.

My mother hugged him, and told him she forgave him. I don't remember how long that embrace lasted, but I and my brother Paulo were in our dining room looking out the window towards our backyard, just wiping the tears from our eyes when this woman tempered in steel noticed us.

Immediately she came to put her arms around us both, squeezing us by her side looking up to the sky, and as loud as her cry could sound she proclaimed to the heavens. "As God is my witness these children will lack nothing". "Lano (what she called my father) please help me. Help us." Then she kneeled down, looked us both in the eyes, and with the assurance only a mother lion can provide to her cubs she said "we are going to be alright!. I have never felt as safe in my mother's arms as I did in that moment. To this day, every time I see Vivian Leigh playing Scarlet O'Hara in the "Gone with the Wind" all I see is my mother and that moment. Things started changing from then on.

4

My mother contributed to the economy of the household by earning a few cents washing my father's co-workers clothes. Scrubbing them furiously to take away the smell and stains from diesel engines, sometimes almost having her nails falling off from the excess of soap and other abrasives.

My father was an Electro-Diesel Tech. I did not learn or know much about him, aside from the fact he was the second youngest of six siblings, three girls and three boys. The most vivid memory I have is that of a gentle but tough guy who on the day he had to be submitted for an urgent surgery to extract his appendix, he drove home about only a couple of hours after waking up from his procedure, against the orders and strongest recommendations of the doctors. He trusted his wife, my mother above all and his recovery was made entirely in the comfort of his home. He was an expert in what the diesel engines have, called the injection pumps. These were particular to heavy vehicles and mainly excavators and bulldozers in general. My father was the person testing these fundamental parts in what was known as 0the testing bench. These machines were used in clearing the African jungle and building new roads. He started this adventure in Luanda the capital of Angola for a limited time and then was transferred to the northern province of Cabinda which is an enclave of Angola. My mother returned to Lisbon with a new baby, my brother Paulo who had been born in Luanda.

When his commission in Cabinda terminated he was hired by an outfit called "The American House" which was braving new worlds and opening new roads.

Again he was overseeing the testing to assure the good performance of these diesel pumps. After one year he was sent to a different area to set up a testing site in a different province. His second born child, my oldest brother, never knew why they left the dry province of Mocamedes, sitting near the desert of Namibia so quickly, and was tempted to believe that it was because of his school; but I heard my mother tell a different story. It so happened that the winds of a revolutionary war were already blowing and even though the guerrilla did not start officially until 1961, an episode appears to have happened in a local cantina. It was the year of 1959. An African man apparently allied with the freedom fighters had gone to drink, late at night and got severely intoxicated. A policeman who was there at the time, warned the bartender that the man had reached his limit and ordered "not to serve him any more".

The man got agitated, he wanted to drink and it was then that the policeman mockingly asked the bartender to get a glass of water, since he wanted to drink. The man repelled the water in horror pleading not to be forced to drink, such despair raised the suspicion of this policeman.

Soon after, he confessed "they" had poisoned the village well. This was an accidental stroke of luck and the first symptom that an armed struggle would soon ensue; to my mother this was enough to have the family pack and leave. As my father looked for a position now further south in Mozambique my mother went back to Lisbon pregnant with me and in order to enable my oldest brother to finish school. My father got the position in the commercial division of a Mercedes Benz franchise. I was born in Lisbon and after the proverbial 6 months waiting period after the birth we all shipped out to LM as it was known (Lourenco Marques) at the time. That is how we made it home.

5

Ilda, my mother, was born in 1920 in a medieval town of the center of Portugal called Coimbra. The oldest daughter of 6, her father was an artisan, a wood restoration worker, employed mostly to restore domes in churches, especially where gold leaf artistry was required. She soon found herself with the added responsibility of aiding in the family's finances. The great depression and the still going recovery effects of the First World War did not leave much to chance and her dreams of becoming a doctor, with six siblings to feed, soon became shattered. She wanted her brothers and sisters to prosper, so she ended up finishing her schooling as a nurse, started working immediately, and with her help her youngest brother became a renowned professor and a historian. The others also advanced successfully in life in different areas. My grandfather, like all older men at a time, facing the prospect of hunger in the family, was a hard man, making sure his children and wife understood the hardship of times in which there was no room for complacency. My mother worked diligently using her compassion for those in need as a purpose to survive now with the prospects of a second world conflict.

Being now under a fascist dictatorship, Salazar the head of state proudly claimed he had not saved Portugal from hunger but he saved it from the war. Portugal became a haven for Nazi intelligences and other activities. One day coming home from work, my mother saw a homeless woman sitting in a cobblestone street, in the rain, with a worn down blanket and no shoes. The rain was cold and coming down heavily but my mother walked home leaving her shoes on this poor woman's feet.

She got home, and immediately, as shoes were an expensive commodity, my grandfather asked her what had happened to them. She simply stated she had given her shoes to someone that really needed them. She was prepared for the severe beating that followed, but I know that her joy for relieving that woman's feet was much bigger than any pain this beating was causing. When my grandfather died, the responsibility of looking after her mother started getting shared by her siblings, who were already old enough, and she could start looking a little after herself. She got married and her African adventure started gaining shape.

6

To the older generation of white Portuguese the concept of passive racism is appalling and unacceptable. Portugal had a somewhat different approach to its colonies. There was always, maybe because of the DNA of the "alma Lusitana" (Portuguese soul), an attempt to defuse the lines between oppression and integration.

The story of the success of Portuguese values and culture in Brazilian society for example, a country about 92 times bigger than the little garden planted by the seaside, can be almost summarized in a symbiotic relationship between repression and a hybrid approach. The Portuguese mingled with the population, sometimes having mixed race marriages with mixed race children. They all became, in a sense, part of one another even though preserving the proverbial social distance between lighter and darker offshoots. The fifties and sixties modern Portuguese colonialists were compassionate people for the major part yes, also because a lot of them had been considered "persona non grata" in the mother land for their opposition to the fascist government.

Many of them, after doing time as political prisoners, enduring terrible conditions, especially dedicated centers of detention, in the most torrid Portuguese colonies such as Guinea and Cape Verde, were mercilessly given the opportunity to live in exile in Mozambique.

So these survivors understood well what oppression was like, but even those that dared not speak against the regime never - surely there were exceptions - were of the opinion that branding a whip or exercise power via physical force, very much the example from our neighbors in South Africa and Rhodesia, was not in consonance with their Christian values, and so just because the access is limited to certain areas, not to give the indigenous population an opportunity for education, keeping them illiterate and serving their masters while being miserably rewarded, was not racism. The blacks were living like that because it was their culture after all. Their way of life even before the Portuguese arrived. Besides, to turn a piece of abandoned land into what became one of the most enticing spots in the world for tourism and for sure one of the most beautiful places in Africa, is a "clear example" of the Portuguese entrepreneurship and love for the land.

This sensitivity to "what might be somewhat wrong" made possible that in all my Mozambique experience I never witnessed drinking fountains or restrooms designated by the color of the skin as in South Africa or North America for instance. There was no argument there. The citizenry however in its defense had a very thin line to toe. The regime was strongly supported by a Portuguese version of the Gestapo. Politics and Religion conversations were off bounds and the press censorship made sure nobody had the audacity to even in thought cross those lines.

7

After my father's death mother had to kick her heels and appeal to the stock pile of steel and fortitude, acquired through the long hardship of her youth and face the fight. As the Portuguese saying goes "it is the habit that makes the monk" and so she started by getting her driver's license. She had been the chief nurse of a very limited medical staff at the local headquarters of the police force. She needed autonomy.

This was a very large facility composed of various buildings, like any police precinct, resembling a military base. Auto shop, arsenal, various offices, a main square and at the bottom of a somewhat steep hill were the medical quarters. Paved with cobblestones was a very wide open way going up towards a more sinister building where the prison was. This was a walk with no shade to shelter from the heat and guarded by well-armed men with nowhere to hide, in case somebody had any ideas. Even though I visited my mother at work many times, I was never allowed to get too close to this building.

To this day I still believe there were among the cells and offices of the commanding offices and personnel, some rooms dedicated to obtaining information from some special detainees. My mother when it came to certain subjects made use of her lioness instincts and kept us at bay. Because of her qualifications or time of service she was attributed a military or paramilitary rank. She was the equivalent of a lieutenant and displayed her brass over her white coat. As I grew older I started to realize, not yet understanding why or how, that this was a special human being respected and admired by everyone black or white, cop or civilian who would, without hesitance, show an unwavering reverence towards her; almost even an unexpected and unwelcome subservience.

8

Being a white citizen in this Africa was easy and sweet at my age or at any age. LM was often crowded with tourists from South Africa, Rhodesia or even many British travelers looking for the African mystery. These shores bathed by a majestic Indian Ocean were loaded with an irresistible appeal. The sea was warm, generous with its waves and marine life. I remember in one particular section of the beach favored by the locals, noticing a diving structure about fifty yards of the beach line, which appeared to have a few wooden poles in a square formation to isolate it from the rest of the ocean. Came to find out it was really intended to be a swimming area away from the shore and the poles were once the support structures for a heavy metallic net so to protect the divers and swimmers from any undesirable visitors. Short lived however was this swimmer's dream since it was soon proven that the net was not strong enough to resist the high tides or the teeth of some very large sharks. It took but a few deadly encounters in a very short span of time for this area to become forbidden to the general public.

Those familiar with the marine fauna in the area needed no further warning neither would try to test their God and defy the elements. There was no coast guard or any kind of police to enforce the directive of "No Swimming". Everyone knew that if you did, you would be on your own. I loved those rich dunes with spikes of tall grass contrasting the green against the white sand and the blue of this wonder. During the low tide, we could just walk on soft muddy ground now uncovered by water not higher than the knee, for an extension of almost a half a mile, digging out clams sometimes the size of our palms, and small shrimp.

In certain areas, around dusk it is possible to hear a strange noise resembling the walk on loose gravel. In a unique spectacle of Mother Nature this is created by hundreds of large red crabs coming out of the water to spend the night on dry ground finding maybe refuge from predators amidst the grass and the dunes. If one waits for the first hours of dawn this phenomenon happens again now in the reverse direction. Every evening fishermen with large fishing rods and specially dedicated reels, hooks and bait would throw their lines in the ocean from the shore, to catch dolphinfish , grouper and many times sharks and rays.

Earlier while some were fishing, indigenous young men would climb with their bare hands and feet tall coconut trees to grab the coconuts and sell them to passersby. Many times as the tide started to recede it would be possible to see in the distance small humps in the water that I discovered later to be the bottoms of indigenous women bent over in the water, their heads fully immersed while digging for clams that they would later sell on the streets. More symbolic was the sale of pineapples sweet as honey, since they were proficuous in the beach dunes. Yes, life was sweet and easy and the seafood abundant. It was normal at the time for the local bars to have the proverbial peanuts replaced with free cooked shrimp when tasting a beer. There was no lack indeed. Leaving the city lines one could have a forty minute drive to the town were really everything as far as the Portuguese dominance started, where once a Regulo (ruler) who was the leader of the local tribes could not resist the powerful Portuguese army. Gungunhana was his name and where his home once existed there was now a monument where the Portuguese officer had him on his knees. This was a privileged location on a plateau with a viewpoint facing the Nkomati River.

I remember with the family making it a frequent trip down by the river line and with the skill of movie stunt driver my oldest brother driving the car atop a very primitive barge.

A very limited number of cars could be placed there at a time, so the weight would not be too overbearing for the locals on the other side of the river who would pull this vessel by the strength of their God given arms using nothing but a set of solid ropes strategically placed in several points of the barge. Talk about understanding the laws of physics without ever seeing what a classroom looks like. During this slow crossing we could just watch, looking at us with only their ears and eyes above the water, a dozen or more hippopotamuses, resembling probably what our facial expressions are like when we visit our butcher shop. The shores of this river were also heavily populated by very large African crocodiles. Later I learned that it was common for that area where humans coexisted with these large animals, to have quite a few becoming prey especially among young children who would not yet have learned all the alarm signs passed from grandparent to parent and subsequently to their children.

When they dared go for a swim in the river this was a true gamble with their lives. Once we arrived at the other side, now we had a good twenty to thirty minute drive on a very muddy trail, towards one of the well-hidden gems of that part of the world. Macaneta beach was a Mecca for fishermen avid to catch some serious sea life. The dunes were inhabited by different species of monkeys, there were surprisingly plenty of Mango trees, and the water amazingly warmer. No one would go in the water once the high tide started to announce itself, in one instance my oldest brother had to pull me violently to land from a wave that I was delighting myself on, with his arm. Time was up. The sound of fishing lines being thrown into the water echoed along the beach like a swarm of mosquitoes.

There are plenty of spots like this along the shores of Mozambique, and for those more inclined for serious game in land the local fauna is nothing to snub your nose at. We had good acquaintances with families whose houses resembled the halls of museums more than private residences. Trophy hunters, very respected and admired by a population and a culture with still so much to learn.

I did not escape this fascination and was often a good agent of propaganda of these "heroes" of the jungle. These were the explorers that would have met Tarzan in person if they ever crossed paths. An entry wall adorned with two enormous elephant tusks, the size of a door, as a portico and not only legs of a glass table but floor ashtrays built out of elephant knees where the plates would be attached by a gold or silver ring. Different heads from Kudo to Zebra, from Buffalo to Lion, different skins adorning either walls or floors. These trophy hunters did this for sport but with the proper connections would also serve the interests of foreign wealthy customers. I cringe now at the thought that at one point in time I was a founding member of their fan club. Life was easy and free, careless and worriless.

The fact that our house was often visited by strange local indigenous people who did not stay long for the visit was intriguing to me. These black men, many times accompanied by their families, would open the 6 foot iron gate that would separate us from the street and would walk up to our backyard, carrying some small livestock of their own.

9

Chicken, ducks and so many times piglets or goats. They would come to bring my mother these offerings, in appreciation for her treating them for free, not only providing them with medication but also with the necessary vaccinations. I find it difficult that the State did not know about this but she was never stopped by the authorities for applying this private medical care that was almost exclusively administered to the white population. She was always being solicited to become these men's children's godmother even though many of them were of the Muslim faith. She denied no one this request and was quite honored to be asked. The men believed that by having her as a godmother, their children would be in a safer place. They all, from different places and ages, Christian or Muslim named her their "mama" a title of respect adapted from the Xironga dialect "mamana", meaning the woman who usually because of her age, my mother was not old enough, and position within the family was the one to be revered. I have no idea how many my mother helped, but the gifts kept coming. It was also intriguing to me that not from the side iron gate but from the front door politely ringing the doorbell, some very well placed in society individuals would come solicit her services.

The core of the issue was not much different, aside from the fact that for being executives of big corporations or ranked military officers as well as members of the police department being white would grant a different access to the same quarters. I can remember one day in which a top executive of a Swedish automobile manufacturer showed up desperate for salvation. She was already waiting for him which tells me he must have called in advance. The doorbell rang loudly and uninterruptedly until my mother ran to open the front door. This man wearing his pajamas and a very expensive looking bathrobe barged in the house screaming in pain. My mother's words to him were only "go lay down there", she meant the living room three seater. Not a minute later she reappears armed with a huge syringe, exposed the man's buttocks and injected him. He stayed there for a few minutes, now almost sleeping, immovable with no pain. Then he would stand up, would thank my mother profusely calling her a God sent and went home. I asked her what had just happened and her answer "Oh ...he has very low tolerance for kidney stone pain". There was also this skinny, very elegant and short officer of the cavalry. He revered her. We followed his career very closely as he was in our house more often than most always needing some kind of assistance either medical or counseling. He started as a captain, then a major and the last I saw of him he had just been promoted to a lieutenant colonel. Always impeccably dressed with uniform and brass, with his khaki pants tucked inside the knee high riding boots. After all the years they had known each other she looked at him as a younger brother, and still he always greeted her by kissing her hand. This guy was an officer with different commanding posts in the front, and had amassed a great spoil of war ivory and ebony artifacts that we know of. I was not definitely going to inquire about what he wanted every time he rang the doorbell or kissed mother's hand either at hello or goodbye. But what tells the most about these visits is the case of a former special operative turned sergeant of the police force who made our family his primary object of protection. He must have owed her a big debt of gratitude. I could not understand what it was but one day it became clear. This man of a very respectable position had impregnated a young black woman.

He was genuinely fond of her but would have lost his position and his reputation - never mind the serious excommunication from his family. His wife and two beautiful teenage daughters would have given him the choice of either having the pregnancy terminated or his life was over, never mind trying to walk his way back into some "semi" graces. The young black lady was obviously defenseless and at the mercy of a white man. He consulted with my mother who showed him what that meant for a poor black woman overpowered and with no solution for life. She probably told him to find a way to own up to a scenario he had created, at no fault of those he loved. This young woman did not at that point stand much of a chance or even sense in life. With her support however a beautiful young mulatto baby was born, and to this man his new and biggest challenge in life was to keep this secret from his family and society in a milieu where everybody knew more or less what was going on. Nowhere else did this young mother have the ability to go but our house for support of all kinds and even to merely socialize as a normal member of society. Many times they came secretly as a couple.

Much later in life as age becomes the great master of understanding wrongdoings, she was finally introduced to his family, but for the longest time the only validation she found as a woman, came from our home. My mother indeed tended to the needy of both classes equally.

10

When I was almost fourteen years old I was given my first motorcycle. The legal age to ride it was precisely fourteen and this was not because of any deserved reward but for practical reasons. We needed to become in a way self-sufficient and as autonomous as possible. It was a vast open city with different demands for white adults especially the ones with busy schedules. That motorcycle that I rode from then on every single day, provided with some of the biggest pleasures I have ever experienced in my young life. Endless rides either with my closest friends or completely alone along the ocean side marginal avenue. Helmets were only used to participate in motorcycle racing so I used to tilt my head slightly towards the sky and allow the gentle warm breeze to clean my mind…..to purify my soul.

Those days taught me the value of stillness, and the practice of the conscious absorption of my surroundings. I could be riding there forever until there was no world left to go. At the bay the sky at sunset turned sometimes purple, sometimes the sun had the tone of a blood orange and the Portuguese often would leave their abodes just to benefit from the healing of these gifts from this blessed piece of earth. They did not mind. They would drive for miles, choose a location and would simply step out of their cars to gaze at the horizon in small deep breaths. This very common ritual became known ironically as the "route of the saddest", since this was one of the richest experiences one could ever have. Not just at sunset but every weekend, the panoramic

places and the marginal road were filled with people and cars eager for this balm from heaven that only Africa can propitiate. The community came together just to enjoy and appreciate the place they called home. I wonder nowadays with the power of a television set how many let it go unimportant, unaware of the beauty escaping through their fingers…..life was indeed sweet and easy, careless and worriless.

11

Everything changed in that month of April 1974. That Wednesday dawned as any other day of the week, as any other Wednesday, but for those my age, we sensed there was an uncertainty in the air. All the papers had in bold Headlines the news of a leftist coup d'état in Portugal.

The military operation orchestrated by a group of career officers later named the "captains of April" took place at the first hours of dawn. The military had taken position in all the government buildings and were about to topple the fascist regime of over 50 years. This bald movement became known as the "carnation revolution", since hardly any shots were fired and casualties were reduced to a minimum. Once the population realized what was going on, massive amounts of people came out to the streets in total support of the military, surrounding the soldiers and the tanks, while placing carnation flowers on the barrels of the machine guns, in a poetic demonstration of will, that no blood needed to be spilled. This was political not a civil war. The mass of people which by their actions practically shielded the soldiers, was what prevented the members of the regime from opening fire in their own defense.

They did not want their name in History to be associated with the blood of civilians. Just like that twenty four hours later a military junta was making an announcement on the local television station that the fascists had been deposed. The ecstasy experienced by the Portuguese in the motherland echoed all around the world. Portugal was seen as a powerhouse in world politics much to the blame of its empire in lands of Africa. I do not know what living under fascist dictatorship was like to the citizens in what was called "the continent", but to us Portuguese-Africans this did not change much of who we were. We were not on the short end of discrimination. We did not go on the streets with demonstrations of joy or shouting words of support for the new people in power. This was news with a different relevance to those forced to live Europe in exile simply for having a different opinion about the government. There were plenty of political savvy people among us, only now revealing themselves to us, due to the new circumstances. However, at the distance of over 6700 miles or almost 11,000 kilometers, all that was happening felt too far away and not as significant to us. Nothing would probably change that much. Or so we thought.

I was one of those whose witness testimony would be limited to very basic knowledge. We knew there was a war going on but the subject was not open for discussion.

We did not have much of any details aside from the fact that close enough to our house there was an army base, from where soldiers would be deployed to the front. We also knew there was another base usually used as the boot camp for new recruits. The majority of these soldiers were drafted in Portugal and shipped to the colonies with an armed conflict going on. Mozambique was only one of three major wars siding with Angola and the Portuguese Guinea. These young men were shipped out across the ocean, never having before left in many cases their rural upbringings, where life was very simple and uncomplicated. More than any memory can bear, many of them kissing their mothers and sisters for the last time on that fatidic day. Leaving the confinements of a European culture rich or poor, to go to a tropical climate was not an easy transition, where the toughness and challenges of the war were often matched by the diseases a tropical rain forest is very proficuous in and for which many vaccinations were not efficient against.

Paludism and cholera were common maladies that these poor young lads learned to confront and in many cases sustain, while still trying to understand how to navigate heavily mined trails and fire coming from all sides of man sized grass, when ambushed by guerrilla fighters.

Many of these God fearing young men did not have enough mental fortitude to stay in this environment for an average of four years, and the outcome of the collapse of their minds or physiques, was in many cases to put an end to their lives prematurely. Not just physically but also mentally crippled was the result for so many others. From where we lived, every time there was a convoy of these young men leaving now the environment of LM to go to the front we could hear the sound of their loud singing from the back of an army truck in a morbid ritual, with lyrics adapted from military martial tunes into songs of goodbye on their way to the port where they would ship out. All that trajectory the sound of these men singing echoed throughout the streets. It took me a while to understand the real impact of what I was seeing atop the open backs of these military trucks, why my grandmother and other women at their passage did not wave back but chose to simply close their eyes in silent prayer and did the sign of the cross across their chest.

Maybe superstition made them believe that if they waved back they were sealing these kids' fate and the sign of the cross was a sign of hope. You don't wave goodbye if you intend to see them again.

12

That morning in April as we were walking into our classrooms we would ask every single teacher what did this mean. The answer was given almost word by word as if teachers had met and prepared a script "well….until now we did not know what was going to happen. Now we will. "- to me and practically all of my classmates and friends this meant what? What was it we did not know and what are we supposed to find out? The fascist regime had done an extraordinary job, reinforced by a ruthless and very efficient Secret Political State Police to curb the curiosity of the citizenry. The war was kept thousands of miles away in the inhospitable regions of the Niassa and Cabo Delgado districts and the North Zambezi regions among others.

The first time I laid eyes on Kalashnikovs was late that year and early 1975 when a contingent of guerrilla freedom fighters started penetrating the capital. The transition government of Portugal had gone through talks to negotiate the cease fire and press conferences with the "terrorists" started to become more frequent. That is when one of the leaders of the liberation forces, who much later became president, revealed himself as a well-educated man in fatigues. Questions by the world press were being asked and his Portuguese translators were of course doing what translators do until the New York Times asked a question. Maybe this was an important one or maybe Chissano did not trust the man translating for him so in a move that caught everyone by surprise this guerilla commander grabbed the microphone and in perfect English told the reporter "I will translate for him this time!" Every English speaking reporter from that moment on had a direct speech answer from the horse's mouth. Why was this unexpected? Because we did not know who these men were. All we had of them was this image of black terrorists violent and uneducated who serving foreign interests declared war on us.

What we had not been told is that these men leading the guerrilla forces had master degrees and doctorates in political sciences, sociology and law, with an academic life completed in some of the most accredited universities not only in Portugal, but in the Soviet Union, La Sorbonne and even Harvard. Over 20 of these young students left their education establishments to go lead in the war against the colonial power. But their soldiers however, looked different to us. Rugged men with eyes that revealed the experience of a life lived in the bush, a constant fight for survival not just against the enemy but against the elements. I had heard tales of some being attacked and eaten either by lions or leopards, not surprised to anyone who had spent more than a few months in Africa. They did not have a uniform dress code. Some had fatigues and berets and boots, others had khakis and tennis shoes on their feet, but what they all had in common was a Kalashnikov across their chest and their right or left index finger caressing the trigger. I do not remember ever seeing a FRELIMO soldier without a weapon. Some of the youngest ones instead of a gun carried a bazooka on their shoulders.

For the peace loving white Portuguese living in a place that would never be decolonized, as promised by their fascist president and government, where the inscription "Here is Portugal", was emblazoned in the black and white mosaic pavement outside the city hall of their beloved capital Lourenco Marques, this felt as the war had invaded their homes disturbing their privacy. Making it even more daunting was the order for immediate withdrawal of the almost 60,000 Portuguese troops, at the dawn of the Lusaka accords which would bring Mozambique to a road of no return towards independence. This would happen around September of 1974 but to some hardline colonialists it was a thought impossible to come to terms with.

13

A morning like so many others of July and August, I had gone downtown with my older brother, to meet a friend of ours. LM was also much known for a particular intersection with two of the most popular cafes on opposite corners, the Scala and the Continental, where passersby often met to spend brief leisure moments with friends discussing the week's most significant events, while sipping on a milkshake or an espresso.

The last regiment of the Commandos Special Force was at the eve of shipping out back to the continent and since they had been ordered to leave their bases they were temporarily relocated to the grounds of the very touristy camping site by the beach. These men had nothing else to wear but their uniforms however were under specific orders not to carry any weapons to avoid the interpretations of a possible act of hostility, and they were the last ones left since they had been the last ones to arrive in Mozambique, to go to the front. Before that took place, the coup happened and they never saw war. It was frequent to see from time to time small groups of these elite troops walking randomly in the city in their fatigues but missing the proverbial war harnesses. That particular morning about a dozen of these warriors decided to take a last stroll within the confinements of the city's downtown, and almost inevitably ended up going to one of these corner cafes. It did not take long before a group of the most hard line Portuguese patrons started, maybe due to the presence of a couple of freedom fighters in normal war attire, provoking them with insults and questions, letting them know how they felt, how cowardly it had been for them to give up on these colonies and their compatriots at their fate, without recourse to the shame and taste of defeat. Tempers started heating up quickly. All the waiters at the Scala cafe were black African men who predictably started feeling the backlash of the confrontation among their patrons. Insults gave way to physical touching and threats, one of the waiters could not take it peacefully to have a former enemy soldier screaming on his face and pushed him back. In seconds one man witnessing all appealed to the "spirit of the commando" in the soldiers and asked them if they would like a ride back to the camping site to get their G3 - the automatic gun used by the Portuguese army. Without hesitation they agreed. The spark of war had been ignited again, with these men now jumping in the back of a Toyota pickup truck, happily driven by a civilian. In our minds at the time, not more than 15 or maybe 20 minutes had passed, when in the middle of a midday city routine with normal traffic and people going on with their lives like me and my brother, this Toyota pickup is speeding down the main artery of the Avenue of the Republica, with commandos somersaulting from the back while opening fire at Frelimo soldiers who had been now called to find out what had happened and to appease the tempers. Chaos ensued in the blink of an eye, with civilians screaming and running for cover and myself and my brother ducking behind the rear fender of a parked car, as this display of hell was unfolding in front of our eyes. It was my first time experiencing the sound of a firefight. No movie production regardless of how technologically advanced their sound system is can faithfully reproduce the sounds and emotions of a real firefight. In the middle of this chaos, a very loud noise resembling a mix of a large piece of glass shattering on top of a zinc sheet deafened us. I looked at my brother looking back at me with a loud ringing in our ears. I could feel how scared he was and so was I. About three inches from his head was the shattered piece of that fender trespassed by a couple of bullets. Immediately he pushed me out of there, crawling behind me into a stairway of a building which had an arcade area connecting both avenues in the front and the back. This arcade was flanked by expensive stores and used to be a popular shopping destination for locals and tourists alike.

The noise was getting louder and the fight drawing closer due to the movement of the soldiers constantly changing positions. There was nowhere to hide. We crawled up to the second story where an insurance company had its offices and my brother's friend worked. All of the sudden like thunder, repeated machine gun fire started coming from the arcade where the echo made it resemble more like shots from a cannon than that of machine guns. I looked around while on the floor behind the counter. All I could see were the faces of men and women screaming in horror and fear covering their ears with their hands. I have no notion how long this fight lasted and how many casualties happened as a consequence of it. But after what it felt like an eternity, the guns silenced and were replaced by some imperceptible voices. People started gradually and slowly getting up but no one dared to leave the confinements of the office. I ventured to one of the windows and to my dismay found myself looking at the mouth of a tank's cannon. Tanks? I had no idea there were tanks involved. This was enough for me to run back to the middle of the room and sit on the floor. An hour or so later we were allowed to leave, guided downstairs by a Frelimo soldier and told to form a line against the wall of the building.

As we for the first time took a glimpse of the destruction around us, I noticed a young soldier picking across the corner of where we were before signaling it was ok for us to cross, and that is when I learned the lesson that you never touch a soldier in combat mode on full alert, scared and who is not seeing it coming. I touched him on his shoulder to ask him where to? This young man jumped as propelled by an electric shock, his finger on the trigger and before he realized it was just us the civilians, I could see his eyes bloodshot, maybe from crying in the middle of the fight. My brother immediately pulled me behind him, apologized and with his hands opened, in a sign of peace, managed to give this young man a few seconds to recover. Fear also makes these men cry after all. Just because we were civilians we did not have the exclusivity of it. Maybe because to him this was still hostile territory and the fact he was a "kalash" carrying Frelimo soldier made him a preferred target. My mind was racing. We learned that one of their youngest fighters who only had a bazooka on him, fired a blind rocket that missed everyone in the middle of the fight but successfully hit a parking lot of a post office, a couple of blocks away, killing a few civilian workers who were trying to flee the zone in their cars. And the anecdotes around that episode kept coming, including one about a young soldier who had reached the end of his commission, about seven months before the coup happened in Portugal. Valdemar suffered from severe PTSD and had never recovered fully from the time he spent in the jungle in the hot zone of Montepuez. We had learned from a couple of his brothers in arms that very close the end of their tour Valdemar was atop a Unimog, a vehicle of choice of the Portuguese army to patrol the "picadas" name given to the trails in the bush, when what should have been a routine assignment took a turn for the worse and forever sealed Valdemar's mental fate. Moving, as was always the case very cautiously, all senses on maximum alert, the eyes scanning the thick bush trying to detect some suspicious movement behind the tall grass, fingers on the trigger of their machine guns, it was common to come across local indigenous people trying to go about their daily business. Unfortunately for those poor African people, their lives presented no other choice but the need to keep living on, regardless of the dangers they, their children and livestock to this day still are exposed to on a daily basis, simply because they do not have the luxury of a pantry in the hut or a fridge where to stock drinking supplies. They have no choice but to leave the men tending to the grain while the women many times carrying their infants in their backs and a large bucket on their heads, walk for a couple of miles through an open war zone to get some water, either for their cooking or the very limited hygiene they can afford. This day the walking traffic coming towards the routine patrol was not that much different, scarcely barefooted women or men casually stepping to the side of the trail to allow the Unimog to pass undisturbed, always making eye contact and waving at the convoy, but suddenly the sergeant leading the platoon gave Valdemar an order he was not prepared to follow. "Shoot her!" he told him, pointing at a young African woman displaying a belly in her late moments of pregnancy. Valdemar did not react to the order, The sergeant ordered the Unimog to stop and yelled again at Valdemar "SHOOT THAT BITCH NOW GOD DAMN' IT! WHAT THE HELL ARE YOU WAITING FOR? I GAVE YOU AN ORDER! AN ORDER! SHOOT HER NOW!" This whole scene must have lasted less than one minute, but to Valdemar it felt like an eternity. Apparently this young black African woman looked straight back at them, realizing what was happening, and stopped, petrified in horror and probably an unwavering defiance. Valdemar couldn't stop staring in full confused panic mode to process what was happening, and incapable to press the trigger. The sergeant raised his G3, aimed at the woman's belly and fired. The explosion that followed blew her body into probably hundreds of pieces scattered all around them through an area of about 30 yards. In all his time in the jungle, this was a new region Valdemar's platoon had been moved to, and he had never seen anything like that before. It was common in that particular zone, women combatants to have their bellies loaded with anti-car and personal mines pretending to be pregnant. As they crossed these patrols, they could mine the trail so they would be hit on their way back to the camps. This sergeant either had great instincts, or had seen this young African woman earlier and she did not have the protuberance of a mother in the late stages of pregnancy. To live among men in a constant war environment in a hostile jungle fighting a guerrilla war, awakens the worst in men and as physiological needs arise, these soldiers would make frequent incursions into these small dwellings, allowing themselves the power to rape or simply pay to take for however brief moments the women that were available. And they were all "available". Maybe that was where the sergeant remembered her from. There is no sense of guilt or common decency in a war where your life span is accounted on an hourly basis, and it was not the fault of these soldiers. The war was to blame and doing it together justified their actions. No one was ever particularly to blame for this. Everyone was in the same boat, the powerful and the defenseless. They had in common the same conscience; not a lack of it, but an acceptance of the fact that in a war, acts of this nature are acts of mercy since the alternative most of the time is the slaughter of these innocent people. It was easy for the revolutionary army to capitalize on the anger and feelings of revenge that the Portuguese army would seed and breed at every incursion; recruiting new combatants like this young African, to whom now life was worth nothing after the loss of their virtue regarded as unnegotiable, was not a hard task to get accomplished. Unassuming, they would easily blend among the most unsuspected and hide their purpose behind the smiles and waves at the passing of every patrol. They became very successful at causing serious casualties among this army of invaders. Valdemar was never able to overcome this moment in his soldier's life. Never recovered completely and remained in a psychiatric ward for the time he had left in his tour of duty. Discharged in due time to return to his civilian life, he could never leave the war behind him. Still haunted by old ghosts he happened to be caught in the thick of the fire fight downtown. Not capable of thinking clearly, he decided to run inside a clothing store and stand by a mannequin on one of the windows, thinking he wouldn't be noticed, exposed to the barrage of bullets flying all around him. Miraculously, and in spite of all the glass shattered around him and several mannequins severely maimed he escaped unscathed. No one can understand what secret the African peoples have developed in their system that immunizes them against the horrors of war. What enables them to function with a relative sense of normalcy in face of inconceivable inhumanity? Even as war inevitably breeds the trivialization of the devalue of human life, with unnecessarily killing of innocents and generalized rape of women regardless of their age. As the authorities tried to get control of the situation and an understanding of what had just unfolded, a group of more resistant Portuguese citizens felt betrayed by a government in the motherland, which in their opinion was gambling with their lives without understanding their African reality, and grew into a sizeable militia which took over the radio waves at the largest radio station in LM. That is when I understood that this signaled the beginning not the end of new and expected bloody confrontations. But what I could not predict was the scale of what could happen and what did not happen.

14

In The suburbs of the city large groups of indigenous men young and old, formed their own civilian force armed with all kinds of weaponry from katanas to axes, machetes and even construction tools such as pics and shovels. They would advance murmuring tribal sounds of war learned from their ancestors and never able to be heard until now, jumping and running forward in a martial cadence at the sound of their voices. There would not be a chance to go back to where they had been just six months before. They went after those of their own race who had cooperated with the oppressor, caught them and publicly and summarily executed them in a way that the message would be sent loud and clear. One of these most feared cooperators was very well known to be an extremely efficient torturer to extract information the Secret Police was looking for. This was a very large African man, morbidly obese who had benefited from some special deference not only from the colonialist authorities but also from some fear inspired reverence among his neighbors. Those who lived close to him knew who he was and what he was doing, catering to his wishes on a "need to" basis regardless of what these were, including as some had revealed afterwards, the pleasures of the flesh involving some other men's wives and rumors say even their young daughters. The Portuguese authorities knew of this, there had been complaints but the relationship was symbiotic, these problems happened in the thick of the suburbs, and who was to say that this was not acceptable? That this was anything other than culture discarded as "their problem, not ours"? The man was a monster in everyone's eyes, but to the colonial government he was their monster. The arrogance and excessive blindness provided by a power fed ego, crippled this man from the ability to anticipate what the signs around him were showing in every corner, at least up until this moment in time, while the transition of power was still in "no man's land". The hate and dread nurtured by those around him for so many years, that fatidic afternoon was replaced with an uncontrollable rage, the need for vengeance and an example to be set for all to see that this man got what he deserved. There would be no room for mercy here. Besides all ties to the old regime, especially while the effect of the most recent events perpetrated by the small force of commandos was still hovering in the air, the possibility that there was a risk for things to go back the way they were was not to be discarded. He was caught, lynched by a multitude of angry neighbors, and his head completely smashed by a pestle, a much needed and preferred tool indigenous women used to amass their grain. His body with a head that resembled more of a deflated soccer ball left bloodied on the street for all to see. Message sent loud and clear and to these people savoring for the first time the flavor of victory, a new sentiment was born, a sense of liberation, a belief that more than freedom looking like a possibility, it was shaping up as the new reality. This area was located by the bullfight arena (aah...yes the Portuguese carried the full weight of their culture with them), and the local airport.

15

Gisela was a beautiful girl. I had met her at a job during summer vacation selling encyclopedias. This was a common activity for young students to earn some money during the summer and she was one of the recruits. She was a year or so older than I was, sixteen going on seventeen. Slender, dark skin with tones of wheat and long brown hair that stretched all the way down to her lower back. One day I was called to my sales manager's office who had shown a keen interest in this Venus with Mozambican blood. She had already been born in Maputo and was a second generation white "Laurentina" name given to the white Portuguese or Portuguese descendants. Her father and mother were the children of white colonists also born there already. Her family had settled in a small farm in the outskirts of LM. Skipping any expected courtesy my manager asked me point blank "what have you done to Gisela?" I had no idea what he was talking about until he revealed to me that when he had given her a special assignment, of course he was trying to lure her into his good graces, the reply he got from her was " i will accept it as long as I do it with Victor". I was not making any sense of this, but it was evident that Gisela had no hesitation in letting him know the only person she would be interested in doing anything with was me. He was probably hoping we would have a normal conversation and I would show him a few tricks he could use but I had none, to his profound disappointment and admiration. "This girl wants you!" he ended with. I never looked at Gisela as such. We were good close friends, but there wasn't on my part any sexual inclination, and being brought up by a strong woman, to look like Venus and being extremely luring to man who could not keep their mouths closed when they met her, sometimes not even capable of holding their spit behind their lips, was not enough for me to start a relationship. And I know how this girl could have been taken without any prospect of a future. "Let some other dog chew on that bone. Our friendship is deeper and too important to dig a stake into it" I thought. I had learned that there had to be some merit in respecting women and that would have to account for something. We grew a lot closer from that day on, she would take me with her to buy lingerie and very skimpy bikinis, would put them on and invite me to take a look and offer my opinion. Obviously she knew what she was doing. Whatever I said would go. I knew nothing about her siblings, she was the oldest of five, and because she lived in the outskirts passing what were now "not recommended" areas to visit, I never had a chance to meet her parents but regardless of the complicated "geography" I am sure her father would guard her with a hunting rifle in hand. As time went on I started looking at her more seriously however, and one day unexpectedly she knocked at my door. I was not sure if I had given her my address, but she showed up. My grandmother living with us at a time opened it, sat her down in what was our office space and came to get me. I had been out in the back. My grandmother was never one to make comments about my friends but that time she broke that code. Her words when she called me, in a way made me think "Vito she said, go for this one. This one is classy!" with a naughty smile in her face. This was the first time I felt some special bond with this woman, the mother of my mother. I went to the office, Gisela was sitting on a couch, very light pink tight jeans with a very tight shirt on. The wheat tone of her skin enhanced her green eyes in a way that no special effects could ever do. I said "hi" kissed her on the cheeks and we went for a walk. In my mind I was starting to make plans. "I think I really like you," I said. "Do you want to be my girlfriend"? She jumped in my arms, she wanted nothing more than this, and I was thinking that there could be something else besides this crush, which by the way would surely grant me some hero status among my peers. She left a couple of hours later, to go home. I was jumping inside with joy and I was gloating. This was the last time I saw her. As the conflicts kept occurring and the convulsions in the suburbs were increasing in intensity, these were now "no access" areas and we were left with no way to communicate. We would fend for ourselves and hope for the best for those dear to us. Deep inside I felt profound sadness and worry. I feared the worst could have happened to this girl whom I had delayed for so long the pleasure of enjoying a relationship with the guy she liked. I felt guilt and remorse. Time eventually pushed her to the back drawer of my memories. Much later and already in Portugal, I learned from a common acquaintance of ours that her parents' farm had been invaded in the aftermath of the downtown fight, and that her father and mother tried to defend themselves with the limited ammunition they had for their hunting rifles. They were decimated, decapitated by katanas and left lying in the property. All without exception in probably an act of angels' mercy. Once the Frelimo platoon came to regain control of the situation they found no one had survived but Gisela. She was barely alive with a deep cut across her head where according to our acquaintance some of her brain mass was exposed to the air. She was placed in permanent care in a vegetative state. Still to this day, I question if she actually survived, and if that was the condition they found her in, so I adopted a position of probable deniability, unaccepting that such a horrific thing could have happened to this beautiful young human being, but there was no way to verify such an account. Too much time had passed. Gisela to this day is the only martyr memory I keep in my heart and still secretly hope that she is alive somewhere with a family of her own delighting the eyes of those who meet her. No civilian unless they had a specific agenda that had to do with killing, would venture these grounds for weeks. And there were plenty of incursions on both sides.

16

There was no particular animosity towards the peace loving Portuguese civilians who were not involved in these militant race motivated skirmishes. There was no residual hate and to most of us black or white, all we wanted was to be able to adapt to the new way of life, in peace and harmony looking towards a new future. The random sound of a machine gun however was still very much alive every day. The Kalashnikovs make a distinct sound, with bursts that resemble the popping of hundreds of champagne bottles. Very distinct from the thunderous sound of the G3 used by the Portuguese army. Leaving our house in the morning, it was normal to hear a fire fight so close that we had to wait until we felt it should be safe to leave. This was done by estimating how long the silence that ensued lasted for. There is an uneasiness in the beginning when one cannot distinguish if the sound is coming from a Kalashnikov or a motorcycle with a loud exhaust pipe. My grandmother, who had endured two great wars, should not have to endure these scenarios again. She did so stoically though, afraid for sure but ready. Many times she was stopped in her tracks doing something as easy as getting a couple of lemons from our very proficuous lemon tree in the backyard. Stone faced, she would go back inside the house and wait. It is amazing how our brains go into autopilot detection when it feels safe to walk and do your shopping, your schooling or socialize with your friends in the middle of the very beginning sparks of a civil war, but we never accepted this to be a reality. After all we were not South Africa or Rhodesia. We were Mozambique. We were different, more compassionate, inclusive and desegregated. We were not the military, not the Portuguese government, and to many of us we also saw ourselves at that moment as victims. One day the machine gun fire got too close to our uncle's house which propelled him to put his family in the car and come to ours for asylum. He was a successful executive in a textile factory, and had built some wealth, but for some reason in that reactive moment all he packed to bring with him was an old grandfather clock with no particular family history. Without even a moment of hesitation he hugged my mother (his sister), and told us they were leaving. Bought his plane tickets and left with his grandfather clock, his clothes and family the next day. His wife and sons had no say in the matter. There has to be a hidden Moliere metaphor in attributing a grandfather clock the statute of "most valuable thing". Time was indeed precious and of the essence. A small mono engine plane with the side door open, would fly at low altitude with a man holding a megaphone, shouting to the population not to pick up objects from the ground, such as what looked to be expensive pens like DuPont, Schaeffer or Montblanc since they had been boogie trapped with explosives strong enough to sever a person's hand or blind them. Creative acts of terrorism every day, at every corner. It was easy to assume that with the beginning of these hostilities some well-established Europeans had already fled the country and something like these expensive objects were simply left behind. The fact that, day on and day off these airplanes would fly at low altitude with these staunch warnings only helped the decision making process of my uncle. We on the other hand were staying put. My mother still had another sibling in the area and people to tend to. We were like so many, feeling as in a bubble shielded by how localized these conflicts were, trying to get our lives back to the usual track, and Kalashnikov or grenade sounds became not only expected but accepted as added features to our daily soundtracks, however the reality of the times was constantly a reminder, hitting us in the face every day. The local hospital had no capacity to attend every wounded and tend to the dead, so bodies started piling up outside for the relatives to be able to come and identify them. This had to be done expeditiously since the heat of Africa accelerates decomposition. I have no recollection of how efficient this open air makeshift morgue was, but aside from the general consternation we all felt, I do not remember any possible scenarios of disease or bodies left to be buried. My mother once again kicked her heels, lit all the candles we had in our house, prayed to all the saints we had living through icons and statuettes and very especially implored for strength from my father. Every day, since she became a widow after that fatal day in October, she prayed to him, only rarely switching from black to a black and white top. She talked to him often, in silence and mostly in prayer. My mother claimed she saw him more than once, sitting in his favorite chair in our living room, one day even going to our dining room windows to close the curtains when the sun was high. She could smell his aftershave from time to time which assured her he was there. I do believe this helped her endure the challenges dropped in her plate by the goddess Fortuna at a time cutting short a life so perfect. I wonder now if some of her expressions of peace I saw at random, either while in our living room or in our porch in the front facing the park, were a testament to those moments.

17

The radical hard liner movement was defeated and there was a sense after the Lusaka accords that the Portuguese who decided to stay were invested in being a part of this new rebuilding effort. We learned a total new vocabulary with words or phrases such as "reactionary", "continuator of the revolution", "militant", "dynamisation group" or "central committee"; "obscurantism and paternalism". We needed to know what this meant. This was the first time we were starting to get acquainted with the leadership of these "terrorists" and their political ideology. We were becoming acquainted with who composed what in our belief was an unorganized army, that in spite of being several times practically destroyed by the Portuguese army as prophesied by our generals and guaranteed by our government, these groups of "bandits" from the bush practicing a "cowardly warfare", invisible through the tall grass and under the shades of the jungle using regular roads travelled by civilians and military alike as mine beds. These insignificant numbers of uneducated jungle raised insurgents that were often bombed with Napalm, were now the ones walking down the streets of the capital, singing patriotic songs - that we had to learn- as victors of an eleven year war against one of the most powerful empires in the world. Who were these Mozambicans? Most to me did not look much different than the population of the south, aside from the fact that some were darker. For the first time we got petrified when coming face to face with a Makua or a Makonde warrior. We had heard war stories about these fierce scary looking giant men. In our imagination they were already scary enough in their tribal attires but now in fatigues and carrying an automatic rifle that image of fear grew one hundred fold. The Makonde tattoo their faces with a special tool made many times of Ebony, which is burned to the point of precision like the blade of a knife sharp enough to carve the skin. These incisions on their faces after they become visible are covered and healed with several oils and plants which give the carvings a dark blue color in contrast with the dark tone of skin. To us, these tribes from the deep north bordering Tanzania were a figment of our imagination until we saw them in person. The Makua from the north of the Zambezi River were also known by their women covering their faces in a white paste. These people were often at the end of a gun barrel of the Portuguese army, maybe because of the fear they inspired, by political reasons or pure ignorance. They were indeed frequent targets and that helped increase their ranks in the guerrilla. We saw plenty of Hollywood productions that would be a nice distraction to us but we knew these were romanticized versions of what was part of our world. When we came face to face with Makua and Makonde we kept our eyebrows raised for a long time. In June 1975 Mozambique became independent and a Popular Republic, with a slogan of unity proclaimed by the supreme commander of the guerrilla, later the first President "Mozambique one Republic of the People from the Rovuma to Maputo". Rovuma the river bordering Tanzania in the North and Maputo the river bordering

South Africa in the South. Maputo became the new name of the capital still known to many nostalgic older souls as LM.

To us, the white youth, not just the white but the Indian and Chinese population of Maputo as well, we had endless curiosity and it felt like being given a book with blank pages in which we had to help write history.

18

"We are sitting on gunpowder barrels which is just what Africa is" was a common opinion among those who had landed on these shores without ever encountering any opposition to their lifestyle besides from within their own kind. But now to my generation there was an aura of excitement with this new movement, a sense of participation and importance. After all the term "continuators" was directed at us and we believed in the inclusivity of all Mozambicans, regardless of ethnicity, color or religion. Though immediate future proved that this was an illusion, at that time we were fully involved, learning about Maoism, Marxism and Leninism while trying to relay a message that the Portuguese citizens were also victims of the deposed regime and the Portuguese forced to fight a war they did not want to fight, becoming crippled and dying for something they did not believe in. I wanted to surf this wave as well, and welcomed the learning of new "words of order", of new revolutionary songs, which in a later moment of reflection did not feel much different than the indoctrination we had been subjected to by the fascist government. Sessions of clarification replaced the classes of moral and religion, part of the mandatory curriculum of our education until the 12th grade. Constantly we were being shown the clandestine publications from the Vietcong filled with pictures with captions such as "the American massacres", curiously enough there was more anti American propaganda at the time than anti colonialist Portugal. From my gang no one had left the country yet so we remained as close and supportive of each other as usual, sharing the emotions in and outside school, with the interesting twist that now we were "reintroduced" to some of our black classmates as being related to many of the leaders of the guerrilla. Some became prominent writers, others to this day still exercising relevant positions in several governmental departments. The supreme commander of the liberation, now nominated president of the new republic, came to town for the first time and gave an inaugural speech in his war attire, as is typical from many of these strong men of Africa. This was new to us, apparently not to most if not all of our suburban neighbors and servants. Rumors had it that there had been a vibrant, very much alive secret network passing information and running sessions of clarification under our noses during the armed conflict. This was done so effectively that even the infamous morbidly obese torturer was kept in the dark. Unusual to us however was to hear the president sing songs from the war. Some of them chilled with a humming resembling the beating of drums. The former Portuguese dictatorship members of the government would not show these displays of patriotism in public ever. I wonder if they had those even in the shower, since it was not proper and perceived as a lack of decorum, exception only allowed to the cardinal who shamelessly put the church at the service of the leader, and was allowed to sing the proverbial hymns during the very few masses he presided, always with the revered blessings and solemn nodding of pious approval from his excellency the President or his excellency the Prime Minister. The fear of excommunication that was in the hands of this man wearing clergy vests was enough to keep a population of strong believers almost in a state of feudal subservience. But this African revolutionary was not like that. I was always very skeptical to say the least of blindfolds of any kind, and while I was mostly interested in what the president was saying in his speech, on one occasion a young academic friend comes rushing in to our table at the cafe where we were listening over the radio, and with the look of a young pup in love who just lost his virginity, asked us with tears of adoration in his eyes - did you guys hear the comrade president sing " Ife Ana Frelimo "?- a momentary lapse of coherence I thought, a moment of stupor and ecstasy incomprehensible to me at the time and I was a big fan of Pink Floyd. So I started treading carefully while learning how to become a member of this revolution without falling in the delusional spiral of fanaticism where our friend appeared to be irretrievably lost.

19

Rui was the point person for clarification regarding what the steps were to become a teacher in the national effort of alphabetization. Ninety eight percent of the natives in Mozambique could not read or write and there were not enough teachers to address this problem which was after the day of independence and even before then, a matter of national security as well as something in which the future of this new nation depended heavily upon, so the solution was to follow the guidelines of war time improvisation and whomever was equipped to teach, could and would teach; this task was now entrusted to young high school students and took place in the local elementary schools. There were plenty, and always at night after the regular school days were over. I walked inside this classroom where Rui was teaching, to learn on the job by observing and assisting with whatever he needed. This was a branding experience for me. Older adults, men and women some of them old enough to be not just my parents but my grandparents, with an indomitable will to learn, embracing a found conscience of the new Mozambique, knowing how important it was to the future of the revolution for them to do this, but with a mixed sentiment between being free and still being taught by young white kids who could very well represent the past. The servitude we were treated with as their young masters of recent memory was still reflected in their ways and we had to urge them all to see us as comrades - their equals. I had no issue with this since my upbringing until then had been one of mutual respect, but in my new revolutionary brother of the gang I still saw some reminiscent colonial spirit when I saw him talking very paternalistically to these older men treating and talking to them sometimes as if they were little toddlers, while getting a gesture of respect in a silent humble nod or slight bow of the head in return. Mixed messages I thought. I had never known about how some of my friends were with their servants, but to my absolute pride and joy almost all had the same philosophy in life that I had. We were in a good place. Yet skirmishes and machine gun fire could be heard every single day still with very rare exceptions. As time went by and we tried to get our routines back to normal, keeping the old pleasures and adapting to new practices, the sacrifices needed in the adjustment to a new society started becoming more visible, almost a common place, and the violence disguised as a requirement for the maintenance of the new order accepted as a necessary evil. To me this seemed not very different than the rhetoric applied by the recently deposed fascist government. Eerie to me was the content of the message the new leadership was promoting via the air waves. Appealing to the commitment of all black and white in the efforts of the recovery- frequently ignoring the other numerous ethnicities - and at the same time challenging the indigenous population to figure out why they had been kept in an illiterate world of their own, why they were working the large farms and reminding them of their condemnation to poverty however true, was in my perception an example of blatant deficiency of good timing. In reality the participation of the white population was very much needed, since the entire country needed their expertise at the time to provide a smooth transition of power and leadership in the existing infrastructure. This was the time when I came to the realization of why Portugal kept these peoples illiterate. Their illiteracy turned them into amorphous pieces of a machine, in a state of eternal dependency of the colonizers. This became self-evident later when the president himself in a public rally, called their attention for the fact they had enough buildings and machinery but no one with enough knowledge to utilize them. They had simply at the time of the revolution missed the big picture. They needed new talent and expertise, and that is why at times to me it was confusing to make sense of a message that had hope and cooperation mixed with invitations to revolt during a critical period of transition. This kept the violence going on, and now some of the ranks in the new military order were starting to show signs of discontent with lack of remuneration and an oblivious existence where a bed to sleep in the barracks, a uniform for clothes and a gun, were the only compensation they could look for. Dissension ensued and different factions started forming. We knew it was only a matter of time before new conflicts broke out. Not long after, we started hearing rumors that large numbers of Africans had tried to take possession of some very wealthy cattle ranches and farms left abandoned, only to be faced with a scenario of dead carcasses and completely destroyed crops by the disgruntled owners fleeing the country making sure none of these invaders benefited from an ounce of their blood sweat and tears shed during their long prosperous life in south east Africa. As propaganda goes those still at odds with the new regime somehow had information that it was the invaders who destroyed everything to send a symbolic message of cutting ties with the oppressors, and as far as the cattle as well as horses chicken and dogs, they killed every single one unlucky enough to have white fur or feather. Many of these cattle ranches had been heavily mined by the fleeing ranchers causing massive casualties among the invaders, an act plainly justifiable in the eyes of the most reluctant to change. This to me was one of the most disconcerting displays of what the madness of war can cause. No soldiers among these victims, certainly none among the livestock.

20

My mother kept going to work as usual tending to the ailments of all in need regardless of skin color. Then the trucks started to show up more frequently, unloading hoards of people, men, women and children, young and old. My mother in the beginning did not ask any questions but her instinct that causes the back of her neck stiff up like a mother lion, came again upon her. Practically every day trucks kept coming, some unloading others came empty only to be loaded up with people taken to unknown destinations. Immediately the lioness moving stealthily like a feline that never left the jungle, approached some people in charge boldly and inquired about what was happening using the old oath of Hippocrates argument which mandated her to screen those new arrivals for the possibility of contagious diseases. The health of those in the police quarters including the leaders in charge was after all her responsibility. Facing the impossibility to argue against this logic allied with a real fear that their military rank would not guarantee them immunity, those in charge including the commander revealed that these were people in need of "re-education". Those leaving were being sent to re-education camps since they had shown to be more resistant to the new system. This they believed, was caused by lack of knowledge so they were going to be shown how to become and what it meant to be a revolutionary. Others were suspected of reactionary practices or of attempted terrorism acts or thoughts. Their fate had yet to be determined. Many of these poor prisoners were never seen again after being sent to camps located thousands of miles away to the North of Mozambique. Mostly these assumptions were based on simple accusations without due process. The concept of due process started the moment they arrived at the jail. Separate from these two groups (the unaccepting ignoring and the precocious terrorists) were religious groups considered dangerous. As far as we knew only Jehovah's Witnesses suffered this persecution and were arrested. Muslims and Catholics were accepted and tolerated. A lot of the fighters were of the Muslim Faith and the massive Christianization of all the Portuguese colonies, had of course converted the majority of the population in the cities as well as their suburbs. Not even during the apex of the colonialism we had witnessed such a terrifying fate given to a particular religious group. Portugal had closed the door to such religious intolerances after the Holy Inquisition. My mother tried to conceal the fear she felt while learning about this, and disguised her indignation with an attitude of the need to look after these people. Without waiting for any special authorization or signed decree, she stormed out of the office of the general command and with resolute steps walked up the bare sunburned terrace towards the dungeons. There were not many, eight to ten cells only she estimated, with a maximum capacity of four prisoners per cell. Approaching the guard and stating she had just left the commander's office while displaying her brass, she asked the man to open the access door to where the prisoners were. What she saw petrified her. There were on average ten, and in some even more persons in each cubicle, mixed between men and women, old and young. The size of the cell with that amount of prisoners inside, made it impossible to lay down or even to sit. My mother saw a few people with signs of sickness but mostly what caught her attention were a few pregnant women some of them in an advanced stage of their pregnancies. She couldn't wait any longer, with a look in her eyes that would provoke the fate of Medusa in anybody daring to stare back at her, went down to the clinic at an accelerated pace, grabbed a thermometer, a blood pressure measuring device, some alcohol and a few pills her instinct suggested would help, closed the clinic behind her and accelerated back up towards the prison. Inside she administered some basic first aid, and was able to get a pulse on what the general condition of the prisoners was. With a bit more information, armed with her first diagnosis, she stormed back to the commander to express her indignation, and to let him know that a lot of those in the cells were at risk of their own lives and could be contaminants to everybody around them. Visibly not happy that she had gained access to the prison, he showed some understanding but made sure she understood they were not to be given special consideration since they were prisoners because of serious accusations brought up against them. My mother obviously roared back at the man and left the office. To her surprise the next morning she had a communication on her desk at the clinic, reinforced only by a soldier she had helped in the past, stating that she was not allowed to go to visit the prisoners anymore and much less provide them with medical assistance unless previously authorized by the commander. To ignore this would place her at the risk of serious consequences. She cried tears of rage but would not be deterred. Asking for this soldier's solidarity she appealed to his better senses and asked him to talk to the jail guards, saying that she would never cause them any trouble but those people in dire need of help would die if she did not medicate them, and on top of it - I think she used this as a convincing argument - they would risk contracting the diseases themselves. This seemed to work. For weeks since then, after the clinic closed the doors at five in the afternoon, sometimes at six where it starts to get really dark at dusk in Africa, and after the commander retired to his quarters, she loaded up her white coat pockets with syringes and other medication and would tend with the guards collusion to the needs of the prisoners. As the practice kept increasing, I am sure the word had passed, that there was this white nurse coming in at night in secret to treat them. To many as they were loaded back in the trucks not to be seen again, this was the last manifestation of respect for their dignity as a human being they had experienced. Her defiance of authority did not come without a price though. It was 3:30 in the morning in early October. We had an enviable collection of old muskets and first world guns adorning the walls of our corridor and office. At least a couple of the muskets had gold engravings over ebony and some the effigy of Queen Maria's I crown. The violent knock on my bedroom window, and then the kitchen door made the whole house shake. Terrified, I jumped out of bed and before I reached the corridor my mother was already walking to the kitchen telling us not to fear and stay calm. As we opened the door three soldiers brandishing their favorite children (the Kalashnikovs), told my mother they needed to research the house since they had received a call saying that we had weapons in our possession. This had been severely forbidden by the revolutionary army and indeed I had a hunting rifle under my bed, the only survivor of a few we had that had been turned into the authorities. The reason that one stayed behind was simply that we had forgotten about it and by the time we realized it had been forgotten the decision was made just to keep it out of sight, since by then it was too late, and the sort of questions it would generate could jeopardize our security. Under a young teenager's bed was not the typical storage place of a gun. I don't remember how it got there but in my younger days since it was not loaded I remember when alone, many times taking position behind the bed and pretending to be a cowboy shooting at the Indians that were threatening the fort. They did not know her at first and only one spoke Portuguese which did not place the odds in our favor. Of course she stepped out of the way and let them in, at the same time she was pointing at her collection including two Mausers with sealed barrels. They believed these were the weapons they had been told about, took them all down and walked out of the house each soldier carrying about a half a dozen. The next day my mother went to her "friend" the commander and told him about what had happened. Definitely he knew about the raid and told her that despite those being collectors' items and not functioning weapons the only way she could have them back was to turn them into a floor lamp. She understood the sarcasm but did not lower her guard. She really turned them into a floor lamp by welding them all together and having electric wire run through the barrels, and got them back. All but the Mausers. My mother never recovered completely from bearing witness to this degradation of human life. When she joined me close to Christmas that year in Portugal, I learned that before the liner filled with Portuguese citizens leaving for the continent set sail, the departure had been delayed. The now general and commander of the southern region of Mozambique, former commander of the police headquarters demanded to go aboard searching for her. The dialogue that ensued was a clear demonstration of what she meant to them, as the commander begged her to reconsider and name a price that would convince her to stay, assuring he would keep the ship on shore until the container with her contents was unloaded in a complete disregard for everybody else's consideration, her words in return were "I saw what you did to your people! There is not enough money in this world to make me be a part of it! Circa sixty thousand Portuguese citizens were given 24 hours to leave Mozambique and did so during that time called the "exodus".

21

A typical day in November in Mozambique has plenty of sunshine and the temperature doesn't go below 73 or 72 degrees Fahrenheit and rarely goes touching 90. It is overall a balm for all the senses and on that November morning I was riding my motorcycle with two of my best friends, JP and Nello. Going down the road where the Town Hall was located, enjoying the breeze and planning to go get some scones baked by the hands of African women who were sitting on sidewalks, displaying them for sale, on top of simple capulanas laid on the ground. That was when I was surprised by my frantic brother who had been looking for me since earlier in the morning. Not wasting time saying hello to my friends his words were "go home now. You are leaving for Lisbon this afternoon at two o'clock!" This happened around 11 in the morning. I never argued with my brother when it came to such capital decisions. After all he always had my interest and safety in mind when the occasions appeared to put me at risk, the latest example being the fire fight downtown of recent memory. I felt lost, paralyzed and did not understand what was happening or how to react. Somehow I knew I had no recourse. I looked back at JP and Nello who had a stunned look in their faces, and my words to them were "please let everybody know!" Turned the motorcycle around and went home. On top of my bed was a medium size suitcase with some of my clothes in it already. Still looking to regain my balance and put my thoughts in order to try and understand what was happening I heard my brother tell me that they had started packing to gain time, but did not know what else I wanted to take so they wanted me to finish packing and to do it now, as quickly as possible. I wanted to speak, to say something…...but my mind was not having any coherent thoughts. Robotically and in silence I practically closed it with what was already inside, hopped in the car with him and was driven to the airport. All the dreams I had of one day getting inside an airplane instead of a liner which was mother's preferred method of Transcontinental voyages, were now dissipated. Vanished in an inexplicable anguish for leaving without warning, everything I had ever known. I felt terribly lonely. Where was my floor, my ground that I used to walk on, to step and jump on? Everything was a blur in time and circumstances, I was floating in the fog of a horrible nightmare. It's the only plausible explanation. It dawned on me I had not said goodbye to my mother, and that did not bother me as much as not being able to hug my best friends, my gang for I did not know if I would ever see them again. Did not even carry a picture with me. My mother would be ok with the absence of my goodbye. She had engineered this from the beginning with my brother and it would be best for her if she did not see me depart, but to my friends this feels like being struck by thunder. I do not remember anything from the moment my brother told me to go home and pack with clarity, up till I started walking the tarmac and up the stairs to the airplane. As I approached the last step to get inside I looked back at the balcony behind us only to see my brother wiping a tear from his face and JP, Nello and Rui, the only ones that were able to make it there. Raised my arm and waved it really slowly. Feeling that maybe this was a life sentence, I walked inside. The airplane was filled with those who unlike me were leaving on their own terms. I was hurting in my core having my roots stretched until that airplane ripped them from me. Looking back in time now there are some mixed feelings with the reality that those roots of mine never left Africa. I would not plant those anywhere else. I would have to grow new ones. I had not realized then how happy I had been until this moment. So many things unlived, so many not cared for helping fill my mind and my heart with a litany of missed opportunities. A profound sadness invaded my whole being. The plane was filled to capacity including with some people I knew, but none of my tribe. I was eager to have this thing lifted off the ground so I could share lack of ground with everybody, but to no effect. My numbness, this emptiness that appropriated my heart, my mind, my soul and even my entire physical body was making its presence felt. How can emptiness feel so heavy? I wanted to cry but instead I think I became angry with nobody I knew and trusted well enough to share my feelings with. Simply decided to close my eyes and do a mental tour of every single corner of my house.

I saw myself in my bedroom, now painted an oily blue from the previous purple. My bed by the window facing a small desk with shelves where I used to do my homework, the walls covered with posters and several stands filled with my collection of several war airplane kits. The air conditioner above the desk gave me so many days of comfort when the temperatures reached enough heat and humidity that one could be sweating in the shower. Walking outside of my personal domain I relived the steps I took thousands, millions of times, to the right first passing by my mother's bedroom with an impeccable bedroom set style Queen Anne made of Teak. The wall at the end of the corridor with yellow color above and a more caramelized tone at the bottom, had a mirror covering it entirely which made the corridor look a lot longer. To the left we faced the main entrance and immediately to the right was the other bedroom that was turned into an office and sometimes a place to hang out. I again remembered Gisela sitting there in her pink jeans waiting to see me. That office was the only room connecting to the front porch, where so many times I sat listening to the radio or the soothing sounds coming from the park across the street. I shared this space more times than I can count with my mother, and would give any of my limbs to be there with her now, promising I had forgiven her for this prank. Stepping back into the corridor going now in reverse, I remembered to the left our living room where most of our African ornaments and collectibles were on display. Many were exquisite ivory works of art made by Chinese artisans such as the seven balls of happiness or the march of the elephants, but others in a more rustic way made by African carvers preserved the integrity of the tusks by simply engraving different animals on them. Then there were the religious representations made of ebony which included masks but also small statuettes icons like the goddess of fertility. We had countless objects strategically placed to make the room more inviting though sometimes looking like a Museum. Our hundreds of books were divided between a book shelf here and the office. Well bound books with gold inscriptions, some of them, on works from Victor Hugo to Camoes from Dostoyevsky to Fernando Pessoa. The living room was separated from the dining room by a hall with what resembled a portico. This dining room was the only area of the house with a bay window looking into our backyard. Exiting it a small walk to where our only bathroom was and immediately to the right, our large kitchen with wall to wall tile as well as the floor with a large table and chairs in the center, where every day I had my breakfasts facing the large kitchen counter where I witnessed some of the best creations the world of gastronomy has to offer. The kitchen had a storm door which was the one usually closed allowing the shade from the back yard blessed with a very large and proficuous lemon tree to cool off the temperature inside. Our backyard had suffered several modifications throughout the years. We had a stone table and benches installed under an awning and to the delight of all that visited we had a large bird cage build that covered the entire back wall which divided our backyard from our neighbors'. We had all kinds of birds deprived from their God given freedom to please our eyes and many of them were killed often by cats, hunting at night, catching those who slept holding on to the netting. Replacement of these beautiful creatures happened more often than I could count but it wasn't much of a challenge. We had become masters in building bird traps. Where a large cement laundry tank was placed limited our confined area, then a small walkway towards our walk or driveway through a smaller gate. The wall across belonging to our neighbor on the other side had a permanent stain of blue and so did the pavement, caused by delicious blueberries that nobody cared for which ripen to the point of dropping off the branches would and call all kinds of birds and bees after the sweetness. I was feeling regret that I allowed so many to go to waste and how I wished I could be stuffing my face with them now. These thoughts gave me some comfort. These people all around me did not know what I was going through and were irritatingly happy to leave a country which was not safe, constantly at war and that did not have anything left for them. That was not my reality. I belonged there, it was my Eden. I was an outsider in that plane. Four hours had passed and we started descending to Nairobi in Kenya. President Kenyatta was a friend of our revolution. Maybe to step there for refueling or whatever needed to be done, was a form of solidarity but it did not matter, I had no idea of what the itinerary was and at this point I did not care. We had to get off the plane and sit in the airport for over three hours. For somebody that never had stepped in an airport as a traveler I now knew two. The Nairobi airport was a lot busier than ours in Maputo. It felt like a beehive at times and at every corner had a soldier in camouflage and a gun even the rest rooms had a couple of resolute looking men in full attire sitting at what appeared to be a reception desk. What is it with Africa and soldiers in fatigues and Kalashnikovs? Was there a place somewhere enjoying peace? It certainly did not feel that way but I could not see anything positive and did not want to give anything a chance regardless of where I looked. After all we were finding out that our stop over was because of a trans board. Once the luggage had been transferred to the new plane we were to board again and retake flight. I kept quiet trying to close my eyes and relive my earliest hours, the moments I had enjoyed with the universe I knew and loved. I imagined myself going around our walkway again and collecting loquats from a large loquat tree in our neighbor's backyard. These were some of the sweetest loquats one could lay our taste buds in. This yellow velvety fruit with a pit shiny as a river pebble, that we would allow to rest in our mouths after swallowing the "meat", until it lost its honey-like flavor. I lost track of how many times I reached out to those branches and just grabbed the lowest hanging fruit. I never climbed this particularly very tall tree, for the simple reason that somewhere halfway through the climb a spider the size of my hands made it her abode and an enormous spider web was proudly displaying her majesty, with silk threads so large and thick that while invisible to many naked eye most of the time when the sunlight hit it from a specific angle it would resemble stained glass from the windows of a church. In my mind this was a portent creature and even though I had made up my mind that it was big enough to eat a bird, I never bothered to find out what particular species she belonged to. I would leave her alone and she appreciated that, I am sure. I would go into my other neighbors' guava pear tree instead. I loved these pears. Hard and green on the outside with a crackling noise when you bit into it, with a red seedy interior. Even when they were not very sweet they were still very pleasant to the palate and when they were sweet sometimes extremely, we would just be there with our eyes closed chewing these gifts from the heavens slowly. Between our lemon tree, the loquat, the guava pears and blueberries, we had enough to sustain ourselves when our appetites were calling. It is not impossible, but I can't remember a time in which my hunger during the day was fulfilled with a sandwich or a light processed snack. This is all I was trying to relive to make sure I did not lose it. Something was telling me that it would be a long time before I would be able to experience the same again and since the departure of my oldest brother, whom I saw as a guardian and a protector to Lisbon to study law, or the death of my father, this was the first time when now older and with a different conscience I learned what it feels like to experience extreme sadness and a profound anger at the same time. It had now been pitch dark for a while when the airhostess made an announcement to the cabin that this was the time for refueling and we were to make a stop in Gabon. To our surprise we were asked to keep the lights off and close the window curtains. As we landed and the plane was refueling which felt like an eternity the heat inside was hard to support. Gabon must have had their temperature at over forty degrees Celsius and those with little children felt the brunt of their complaining which they generously shared with everyone on board. It was strange that when we asked the air hostess why the need to have the light off and no air conditioning we got evasive answers or an attempt to put our minds at ease, but we on board were Africans and could read the signs better than any tarot deck reader, so eventually a lot of us, myself included moved the curtains slightly to the side to take a sneak peek at what was going on outside, only to see continuous flashes of light which revealed to us that there was some kind of a conflict in the distance. Immediately we were commenting with one another there was a war outside and later somebody told us that the plane had landed, been refueled and resumed the flight in a blackout to prevent it from becoming an unintended target, strange nevertheless since I have to this day not found any record or news regarding a conflict either in Gabon or its neighbors at that time. But again to us this was all possible, the proverbial gunpowder barrel analogy. I got tired, exhausted with my thoughts, my grief and slept for a while, until a bright sunlight hitting my window woke me up. Daylight was happening, I looked outside and saw this enormous creamy yellow shade underneath that extended for as long as we could see from the air. This desolate view of the Sahara desert gave me something to distract my mind and deviate my thoughts. I welcomed it. Soon we would cross the time zone!

22

Can't remember much from that point on until we're told to "fasten your seatbelts" on our approach to the airport of Portela in Lisbon. A lot on board were getting excited and there were smiles, laughter and exciting comments from most of the passengers. I did not care. Did not bother seeing Lisbon from the air on the approach. This felt like I was being led to walk a plank with no chance to walk back. This was a moment of "consummatum est" but with no joy of accomplishment. This was a feeling of resignation. There was not a lot of complication that I can remember with customs, after all we were Portuguese citizens and the protocol had been established, so I simply grabbed my halfway filled suitcase and followed the herd of travelers towards the outside. Coming from the beginning of what we used to call summer in Africa with days touching sometimes ninety Fahrenheit I was not dressed accordingly to face the endings of a fall season in Europe and the beginning of what some question to be a harsh winter. Portugal has a moderate climate compared to the rest of Europe aside from the rare exceptions of the countries bathed by the Mediterranean which also graced the southern shores of Portugal. The temperature was touching fifty five, and in Africa when the thermometers were flirting with the low sixties, we would bundle ourselves up with turtlenecks and heavy jackets, mostly imported since this was not a popular garment around those stops. When the doors opened I crossed them in this improvised walkway roped on both sides and stepped towards the outside. None of this felt natural. All I could think of was to see my brother and to my surprise my cousin who was already living there. To see them with a smile from ear to ear when they saw me, a genuine display of welcoming joy, I felt some relief but could not utter any words that make sense aside from the proverbial hellos and answers to "how was your trip?" I could have talked about that for hours but now I was trying to see where I was, and what this new place looked like. It was raining, and in those days Lisbon was not pretty in the rain. It took me a long time to see some beauty in this Lisbon that was poisoning itself to become my home for a long while. That drive to where I was going to meet some of my family for the first time was not exciting or pleasant. This city was dark, wet and extremely unattractive, just a few hours before I had left the bright sunshine of a warm piece of paradise bathed by the Indian Ocean. I heard my brother and cousin talking in a very animated way but was not interested in listening, just preferring to stay lost in my thoughts and the memories of what I had left behind, again fearful of the unknown, none of this had been my choice. These dark cobblestone roads with trolley lines lacing all the streets of old Lisbon were a different world. Ugly and undesirable. My aunt who became my host in the beginning of my acquaintance with this new kind of civilization lived in an old apartment in the first floor (the first one was called the ground floor so the second in our understanding was actually their first), of a very privileged location across from the presidential palace, a small park and walking distance to the Tagus River. The rooms were vast with very high ceilings characteristic of constructions from the turn of the century maybe even earlier than that, but as I walked in and while being warmly welcomed by everyone, I felt like a new species who became the attraction of the local zoo. Aside from those who knew me everyone else was just staring, and not knowing what to ask. Extremely curious for sure, they really did not know how to initiate a conversation maybe because they were not expecting someone that looked like me with my hair over my shoulder and bell bottom jeans, to be a characteristic specimen from the African Portuguese. Today I find this place precious and priceless with small iron cast rail balconies but at the time the first thing that caught my full attention in that living room was a very small screen of a black and white television. In those days the Portuguese were granted daily television broadcasts between seven PM and twelve PM, with the exception of the weekends when it would be on the air for twelve hours on Saturday and earlier on Sundays for the obligatory broadcast of the Sunday mass. I was fascinated by this object, my heart jumping inside, in anticipation hardly waiting for it to be turned on. In the meantime my new found family was curious however awkwardly silent and careful with their behavior towards me. Then at about six o'clock this slightly older girl walked in the room. She lived with an aunt of mine in a next door alley and was committed to a very nice young gentleman who worked at a local pastry shop. They had unofficially become engaged whatever that meant, and to my African upbringing this did not mean a thing. She had a strange appeal, pretty face, very nice smile and ebony like hair and eyes. I could sense the spark in her eyes when she saw me and said "hi". Things all of the sudden became a bit more bearable, more interesting. An unexpected but welcome distraction. To her I carried this mysterious aura of a prince coming from a far away and strange land with crocodiles in our backyards and where we often would wrestle with lions roaming free in our streets. The thrill of the unknown. A head to be put on a wall I thought. She was pretty in spite of her sibilant northern accent that I found ridiculous, irritating and almost unacceptable to live with, but she was older, pretty and definitely sure of herself, certain of her experience and I was prey. I felt a bit tingly for the first time since I was told to go home and pack. I needed to drown my anguish somewhere, somehow and Isabel felt just right. I didn't even mind when she invited me to go to the movies with her, my first time going to the movies in Lisbon, only to find out she was showing me to her friends. At one point she touched my face to turn it towards her two girlfriends and asked them "isn't this a beautiful face?" That felt good but extremely awkward, for some reason even when we set to watch the movie, really leaning towards each other and she grabbed my hand. I could not cross that threshold of breaking the values of a family that had just opened their doors to me. I let myself go with this wave of passion that I was sensing coming from Isabel, but did work as hard as possible not to allow ourselves to get to the next step. One morning my cousin (the one that placed his finger in my face upon the death of my father), who was a protégé of my aunt, whom in turn had Isabel as a living guest in her house for years, called me to the side and in a very father like manner went through this entire rhetoric how he understood the urges of the age, but to be careful since Isabel was committed and her fiancé was also from the neighborhood. I don't know how he knew or what signs gave it away but it was apparent that everybody knew and I still to this day am completely unaware if there was something I did to give it away. Or did she? For the first two weeks after my arrival, to ease the burden on a crowded house with my brother on vacation before returning to Africa, we stayed at an apartment my cousin had rented in a town of the outskirts called Amadora. He lived on one of the upper floors of a building in a very dark alley. My brother's priority to my displeasure was to get me enrolled in school. I was not looking forward to it, but he did without delay, to teach me a lesson in survival and how to fend for myself - I owe some of my survival instincts to this day to his merciless teachings- he showed me from a crack of a window, where the bus stop was at the end of this dark slippery cobblestone paved road. He gave me the time the bus would come, told me what to look for at my destination and which hill to climb to find my school. I didn't even know the currency of the country yet but had to figure it out by myself which I did by asking the ticket collector what coins I should give him to pay for the ticket, trusting the honesty of a complete stranger now aware of my vulnerability. Very early the next morning, he watched me from above as I walked to the bus stop, in the rain trying to make sense again of how to deal with this unearthly cold.

23

I had only been in Portugal for a little time, and realized the only way for me to survive with my sanity intact was to leave my "instinct mode" and try to give it a chance. This was however easier said than done. There was an undeniable appeal in these European capitals that

I was finding hard to discover but I started to come to the conclusion that I may have been the problem, not the country itself. I had to start by looking deeply into the History that was surrounding me at all times, the birth of everything I knew that pertained to my nationality, and lastly at the people and the customs. Between Portugal and Mozambique there were some similarities, though Angola was a lot closer to what Europeans were like than we were. Angola was bathed by the Atlantic, and even in the rivalry (it is true that we the Africans competed in what it meant to be the "real Africans"), we always sensed that it was easier for Angolans to welcome the European way of life than it was for us. They wanted to be in Europe while in Africa. We were proud of our African "heritage". We were on an opposite coast, much farther away and easily influenced by the South African even the Australian way of life than that of Europe. Our ocean was different, our neighbors were Africans "to stay". We were much more isolated from the "continent" than our brothers from Angola or Guinea. But the fact that we were all buffeted by the waves of these oceans however different, gave us a commonality that went beyond our language and cultures. Portugal had more sunlight than any other country in that part of the World, the Atlantic at the West and Mediterranean in the South. Throughout their History the Portuguese could never resist for long the seduction that the sea opened before them had to offer. What we know the world to be today is essentially owed to the bravery of the Portuguese sailors in the beginning of the fifteenth century who through the later part of the century that followed gave "new worlds to the world". The proximity through the Mediterranean provided a short crossing between Algarve and Casablanca in Morocco for instance, which is less than 250 miles away. Africa was the perfect gate way and the intriguing exoticism of India was like a merciless siren luring the defenseless sailor into her domain. We in Mozambique were very far from this reality, with a totally different mentality and way of life. The Portuguese colonists of Mozambique sought to be different than their fellow countrymen stretched through other colonies of the black continent. I do not believe this was intentional, I never had this ingrained in my mind, but our demeanor was noticeably different. We had adopted the mentality and "savoir faire" of the British and Dutch in our neighboring countries, with the exception of the severity of how they saw and dealt with the peoples they colonized. To survive in my new home I had to work on my tolerance level or else there was no light at the end of the tunnel for me.

24

Lisbon has a coffee shop, a restaurant or a bakery at practically every corner. I had to explore these staples of the culture myself, as they were so common no one I met could spike my curiosity. To the locals, the extraordinary beauty of a 1501 late gothic Monastery of the Jeronimos, which is now classified as UNESCO world heritage site - one of many in the country - was a common place monument and in many cases I believe that the recent experience of fifty years of oppression under a fascist regime friendly to Hitler, Franco and Mussolini robbed this people generous and affable in nature, from the ability to pause and reflect upon the beauty and richness of their culture and History. Everything was identified with the old regime and it took a long time for them to wake from the stupor of obscurantism that we in Mozambique had learned about in a very short period of time with the revolution. These people had no reason to be sad in my view but they were. Profoundly. They had been left behind in their own self-development even though Portugal was the sixth world power at the time, fruit of the immense riches flowing in from Africa , Brazil and the Orient until the Famous "shout from the Ipiranga River" in Brazil in 1822, which dictated the first step towards the rupture with Portugal to become an independent nation, and the revolution in India that costed quite a few lives of Indian revolutionaries and Portuguese soldiers, at the service of the regime which resisted for a lot longer than conceivable the transfer of powers to Indian rule. But other autonomous Portuguese territories still remained including Macau, and of course the African colonies of Mozambique, Angola, Guinea Cape Verde and the islands of Sao Tome and Principe. For a country smaller than the state of Pennsylvania with an area of only about 36,000 square miles, this was no small deed. It should not be difficult for us to try and get an approximate idea of what kind of repression must be exercised to maintain such power for so long. But the definition given by the most notorious poet in the Portuguese literature, Luis de Camoes that the Portuguese are a gentle people with gentle customs, may also be an acceptable explanation for the time it took them to overthrow the regime. I needed to find out what defined me as a Portuguese citizen, and so far I was not getting very far. There was a sense of loss permanently establishing residency in my mind. I needed to learn a completely new slang. We had the same language with a plethora of new "dialects". It felt as if we were speaking the same language but not able to communicate; because of all the different influences in the entire Portuguese territory the differences were distinguishable not just in the accents but in their own lingo as well. On the same token, later and gradually as more and more "Africans" were arriving, our own African slangs and lingo were in time starting to infiltrate and become part of the new lexicon. One of the hardest things a newcomer faces while integrating a different society, with a completely different way of life, is to adopt this way as his or her own. The survival instinct causes one to preserve what one knows and build with that knowledge a wall that resists and hinders a faster integration, which could in reality be beneficial to everyone, however that was not what our perception dictated. In the beginning we humbly accepted the hospitality of our motherland but also believed with a defiant arrogance that we knew better and had plenty of stories to tell and to substantiate our cause.

25

Slowly however, a new and crude reality was waiting for us, a general sentiment among the continental Portuguese that had been brewing for a while, born of a long repressed feeling of envy and dislike, for missing opportunities denied to those in Portugal who never had the opportunity to venture into African lands in search of a better life. The ever growing resentment and declared despise they felt for the African Portuguese quickly dubbed as "returnees", was patented everywhere, we dared to declare where we had come from. In their perception and especially during this new phase of enlightenment during the revolutionary times with the resurgence of very powerful political parties such as the communist, the socialist and the social democrats, the Maoists and every single more radical faction one can think of, the Portuguese going through a new transformation that allowed them a much better knowledge about social injustices and a thirst for reeducation, were very reluctant to welcome with open arms the new wave of people dislocated by a war caused in part by their permanence in such lands. "It wasn't your land, you should not have been there exploiting the Negroes" was only one of the very many epitaphs we were graced with when looking for help, applying for a job or in my case enrolling in a school. They were totally ignorant, but we were seen as colonialists, exploiters getting rich at the expense of poor Africans that did not see much of an improvement in their lives as we were prospering. And we were given, translated in articles of all sorts in some press, along with the finger pointing and public displays of disgust, the burden of carrying over our shoulders the blame of the Portuguese young sons deaths, forced to go kill, get crippled and die to protect us undeserving of such a sacrifice. This was exactly the same rhetoric we had heard and experienced coming from the revolutionary movements that were now in power where we had come from. All of a sudden we realized what had resulted in our lives. We had gone from being white Europeans in Africa, to becoming white Africans in Europe. And all of it within the confinements and borders of our birth country(ies). What made it in the beginning tolerable to us was the fact that little by little we were meeting new Africans that kept arriving in large numbers each day. Almost feeling as citizens with no land, now we had to be united and leave behind our old rivalries, and realize that in our homeland we could not be Angolans or Mozambicans, but necessity and survival demanded that we became simply Africans and Portuguese. It became fundamental to our existence. Our newly found survival mechanism. Soon the entrepreneurial spirit of the African Portuguese rose to the surface and we started using our experience from facing harsher beginnings in strange lands to strive in this one.

26

In the period when I was anxiously waiting for my mother and brother to reunite with me, I lived with my cousin, uncle and aunt in this historic apartment across from the presidential palace. I saw the rituals of a horse mounted military band called the "charanga" which is still believed to be the only in the world able to play while galloping. These band members exert a mutual respect between them and their mount. The epithet on their wall states this clearly "The horseman that exceeds himself towards his mount loses the right to be obeyed!" The Solemn Changing of the Guard that happens with pomp and circumstance at the National Palace of Belem, is often described as one of the most beautiful military ceremonies of its kind in the world, clad with great symbolism and tradition. From the small balconies with forged iron parapets I witnessed many and every single time felt a deep sense of pride in such a tradition. I slept in the same bed with my cousin who was approximately my age, an arrangement that did not satisfy my minimum standards of privacy, but gave me the opportunity in this strange intimacy to talk about how different we were in so many ways which started to provide me with a doorway to integrate this new society. There was no turning back, and here in this bedroom, I started feeling for the first time a bit at ease. The Portuguese are very formal, very subservient to what others think of their behavior in public, they carry with them everywhere they go a mental guide of what to say, how to dress and what utensils to put in each hand while eating. In Africa we were very polite but carried ourselves with a lot more casual and friendly demeanor. If we crossed people on the street even those we did not know, it was common to smile, nod our heads in a tacit salute or to voice our wishes of a "good day" or "good afternoon" simply a "hello" would many times suffice. If we did that in Lisbon the person on the receiving end of such a courtesy would look back angrily at you and ask "where do I know you from"? This was one of the strangest discoveries we Africans came in contact with that needed an immediate adjustment and to this day, we still find that to be a staple of how differently we grew as peoples. Lisbon has an undeniable charm, but at the time it felt cold, dark and distant from the sunshiny days of the Indian Ocean shores, even though the estuary of the Tagus River and the Atlantic in which it flows laces the shore line of this European capital, with the westernmost point of mainland Europe all in a daring dance to defy the modern Portuguese to emulate their ancestors and venture towards unseen, even yet to be invented destinies. Among the newly allowed libertine practices (products of the revolution), which proliferated the magazine stands with explicit covers out in the open of pornographic publications, laying side by side with the most serious newspapers of the world, were the very old curved by the price paid for living in poverty, rural citizens still carrying heavy baskets on their heads loaded with small farm grown goods to be sold in the most popular squares of the capital. Old men and women all dressed in black, the men with wrinkled suits and worn out shoes, wearing black old fedoras and white dress shirts holding half of a cigarette in the corner of their mouths, women in long heavy skirts and shirts with head covering scarves, thick white socks and old shoes wearing wrinkles carved in their faces, as a result of work suffered under the sun for hours on end. I remember looking at them and wondering why were they always looking so harsh? If they only knew about the joy always manifested by those African women under a condition of exploited, who used to populate the sidewalks of old LM, laying their Kapulanas on the ground to be used as table cloths to display and sell the charbroiled corn, the ripe mangos or the scones made by their own hands with primitive tools invented by them, many times singing African songs in spontaneous acapellas. These Kapulanas used afterwards as either a wrap-around skirt or in most cases as the baby carriers on their backs. In my perspective their fates though with slight differences were not that much different, so the only explanation had to be in my analysis the weather - one could not be unhappy when one does not have to face the rigors of a winter in Europe with scarce means of sustenance. I came to the realization that the somber demeanor of these rural men and women was because Portuguese people were just simply unhappy. I discovered that those in fishing villages in their traditional attires barefooted in land as in water, had the same wrinkle tattooed faces not by choice or as a rite of passage as in the Makonde people, but that was the card life had dealt them. They appeared resigned to their fate of an endless, merciless brutal life of work to survive. In the beginning I used to walk still only rarely, on these streets and that was all that came to my mind. How ugly and dystopian these people were. And in our midst while fighting perceptions, facing all kinds of push back and verbal aggression, seeing the demonstrations of hate and unwelcoming sites, our joy and resolution would drive them into more madness but above all there was a perplexity, a lack of understanding of how idiotically happy and even daringly hopeful we were. Not my case though still on the lookout for a silver lining among these post revolution times. My mother, brother and my new sister in law finally arrived in Lisbon to my relief.

27

My brother had married this girl from Malawi. She was not really pretty but had jade bright green eyes which would contrast with the dark tone of her skin. She was a mulata. Anita had a captivating smile impossible not to notice. Immediately she fell in the good graces of my uncle who was fascinated by the exotic beauty of this African young woman. He was not a man of many words towards me, his wife or those closer to him but every time Anita smiled he could not hold himself back. That probably by osmosis made him more conversational with me, as I became kind of her younger brother. We ended up sharing the love only brothers and sisters in law understand. The apartment was not big enough for three more adults so for a period of about 3 more months, I stayed in the same place and they found lodging somewhere else. In the meantime my mother was coming to find out that what the Portuguese government had promised to the government employees of the colonies regarding their compensation, was not to be fulfilled. It was common during those times of chaotic temporary provisional governments to blame the revolution for promising what they could not keep. This caused her an enormous apprehension but again like a lioness in times of the dry season when food does not abound to feed herself and her cubs, she grabbed the phone and got herself on the trolley, the bus and the train and visited every single government office to claim her rights and make her voice heard. She had to fight and now without knowing what weapons were available to her or what field of battle she was dragged to. Every single day, week after week, she did this. She left no stone unturned and the times to spend with the family she was reunited with after decades of distance, were not fully enjoyed as her mind was imprisoned by what needed to be done next to assure she was not just a body but a person with a written guarantee of placement after leaving a different Portuguese territory. To no avail. The records they claimed, had disappeared maybe because of "the new revolutionary people in place". All the years of service given to the fascist government were now erased from her curriculum. There was no consideration for her pension, her prospects completely destroyed, and the tent she had built without a roof. She knew then, that deep in her mind she would have a new future even at that age, but as far as the present she could not hide the look in her face while scanning the horizon surrounding her and worrying where the new gazelle would come from to feed her cubs. Fortunately she had a faithful friend, a true unconditional friend. A white handyman man, older than her, whom in many situations she relied on for many chores that required that special ability that some have, to look at any kind of malfunctioning appliance or a piece of wood and know what to build or how to fix it. Sal was a simple man, with a humility the size of his heart. This relationship was a mystery to all of us, to his wife, sister in law and daughter alike (they lived together), and not to my surprise he and his family had shipped out on the same boat and of course he looked for a place in a boarding house near where my mother had stayed. This gave her some sense of comfort, a reliable back up. With her children and Sal close by, there was no stopping her now. Much to her disappointment, she had no alternative but to swallow her pride and look for help from her brothers, those who had always depended on her, and since they were all in Coimbra not Lisbon this was not an easy decision, but she was resolute and they did not have short memories, so gladly opened their arms to her. They were all - thanks to her and had not forgotten - very well established in life, especially the one immediately after her who had his own private clinic in partnership with some of the most sounding names in Coimbra's medical field. She had to bow her head, swallow, that majestic pride only a lioness understands when she has to hand out her leadership to an alpha male, and accept the offer. She would be one of his assistant nurses in the surgery ward of the clinic, but I in particular was not happy with this prospect. The body of water that bathed Lisbon gave me a sense of escapism that I knew I would not have in a medieval town from the center of Portugal. I was not ready to move again. She understood my reluctance, but higher values were at stake and my uncle's apartment was not my idea of a perfect destination to start over. Once again she called upon her reliant friend who would throw himself into the depths of Dante's inferno if she told him she needed something from there. Both started house hunting especially looking into what was known as "the Estoril line". This was basically the coast of Lisbon, town after town of shoreline with affluent and some slightly less affluent areas, but growing in the interest of these newcomers who had lived most of their lives by the seaside. One afternoon in the middle of March a little less than three months after she stepped off that liner, she came to my hosts and said, "I found a place for us". She had chosen a very coastal sympathetic town called Oeiras, situated about 11 miles from the tip of Cascais, about 14 of Lisbon and less than 4 miles from Belem. Perfect for us, while she was relocated to Coimbra for work. We finally had new ground to walk on.

28

Located on the right river bank of the Tagus with an area of less than 18 square miles Oeiras benefited from a temperate maritime climate, and with lots of attractive gardens, parks and beaches it was more than suitable for our usual outdoor activities so characteristic of the African way of life. It is and has been for centuries considered an autonomous economic pole, one of the most developed and richest counties in the Iberian Peninsula presently and even in Europe. We did not know or care at the time about the stats of the region. It's quality of life is notorious and recognized globally, with a landscape of valleys, streams and higher areas. It was not by accident that the 1st Marquis of Pombal in the 18th century became the first Count of Oeiras. He was indeed the Secretary of the State of Internal Affairs of the kingdom during the government of King Joseph I and who the most prominent minister became probably in the kingdom, known for his swift leadership in the aftermath of the Lisbon earthquake in 1755. I lost count of how many times I heard my mother quote the Marquis, after the earthquake when the people were in a permanent state of mourning and practically all of downtown XVIII century Lisbon was decimated, he is known to say "we will mourn the dead in due time but first we need to tend to the living" which she used to illustrate how in life sometimes practicality takes precedence over feelings. "Act now, cry later"! The Marquis made Oeiras his official residence. Oeiras seemed fitting with its natural light not blocked by tall buildings or the convulsion of big cities. As it is common in Portugal most of the residential landscape is composed of a system of apartment buildings. Oeiras had plenty of them but no taller than six or seven floors, and outside of the historic district of the town, most were built upon small hills with a privileged view of the Tagus from where one could experience at dusk the serene breeze coming from the ocean. It looked more familiar, friendlier and it exhaled hope at every turn. This small coastal town was loaded with possibilities, maybe even a repurpose for those of us who had left roots behind and felt still as in the middle of a shipwreck fighting to stay afloat amid stormy waves, trying to reach the shore that appeared to fade with each stroke. For the first time in a long time, taking a deep breath and allowing our eyes to scan the horizon again became a reality. It wasn't anymore impossible from that moment on to roll up our sleeves and be allowed to dream again. As I was venturing my new steps in this new unknown unconquered territory, I came to find that almost all of the dwellers of my neighborhood in this little portion of land were like us returnees from Africa. We all had the same instinct, maybe made more acute by so many palm trees that adorned the gardens of the Marquis' Palace and some of the public parks of this small European village. We realized once again that after all, Mozambicans, Angolans and Cape Verdeans were not that much different, and our stories with all the different nuances had the same old plot. We had a lot to share. Yes!!!!! We were all Africans now welded together around the same ideal. Maybe even with a better understanding of the cost discrimination carried to survive in the land of "His Majesty"! To show the locals that we did not get rich without dripping countless tears of sweat and blood. And without servants the fighting spirit of the Lusitanian blood that had conquered the world during the maritime discoveries had now an opportunity to manifest itself once again within our own borders; we were not claiming anything other than our own dignity and there was a lesson to be taught. Progress takes courage and initiative. Never mind that now we did not have our African servants to cater to our mundane pleasures. Besides this piece of the coast felt more than alien territory now. In a time of crisis and despair we found a new family, hopped on board of this yet fragile vessel, grabbed our oars and started rowing towards the unknown but with an indomitable spirit that we would not stop until we reached our destiny. "What made us successful in Africa would make us great in Europe" the more nostalgic yet resolute among us claimed the prophecy would be. Nothing would deter or stop us in our quest regardless of our age or gender. Instead of tall grass in the bush we would now cut through concrete. Instead of katanas we would now use jackhammers and ingenuity but we would prevail. This dream, allowed by our God given right to fantasy, proved to be easier said than done. Many of these heralds of the new Portuguese African spirit were older and incapable of facing on their own the challenges that a new life in a European culture presented them, not after so many decades where competition was nonexistent, where the benefits of a solidarity based on race was a reality, and white domestic servants were expensive and not submissive to the wishes and intricacies of their bosses. Not masters. But there was clearly an opportunity to develop a new solidarity. So here I was, getting settled sharing the same fate as so many of my newfound neighbors. There is undoubted strength in sharing adversity. That first night I walked to my kitchen window which had a small view of where the Tagus meets the Atlantic. I could not hear the ocean from that distance but could at times smell it when the wind blew in our favor. I thought "it could definitely be a lot worse than this", turned back to my room, laid in my bed and remembered staying with my eyes open thinking how time moves so slowly since I had left Africa. My friends, my buddies, my childhood where were they? I wanted to fall asleep thinking of them Marisa, Carla, Fernanda, Sandra, JP, Rui, Virgil, Sergio, Paul, so many more I was almost losing count. There was nothing I wouldn't do to be able to see or at least talk to them now, letting them know how sad I was for not having them with me, how angry I was that my country had pledged a war without a purpose that placed all of us in this predicament. As night kept falling darker I was struck by a sudden realization. There was no noise outside, no city agitation as i had experienced while in Belem or Amadora. There was in a way a very familiar silence that I had missed for so long now, and most importantly, there was no sound of sporadic machine gun fire. How could I have forgotten how sacred the silence of the night is? Invaded by a deep serenity, a true sense of peace that I had long lost, I closed my eyes and fell asleep.

29

Even for someone my age with minimum responsibility if any at all, this period of adjustment required some serious mental agility. Stepping outside of my building to get acquainted with my surroundings, I had a piece of good news. Somebody that used to live in my neighborhood in Maputo had moved into my building a couple of floors below mine. This was extremely comfortable to both of us since most of the people in our age group that were starting to show up or moving in were from Angola, and they had some commonality we did not, which could very possibly hinder our approach of "all Africans" with fairness and equal dependency on one another. But we managed to make new acquaintances and some became close friends. In a little time the differences started to be less evident. Diagonally across from our apartment complexes, there was a small street with few stores, in a strip mall format. All but one store owner had come from Africa so now we had some commercial structure that could identify with us. There was a pool hall with a cafe snack bar, a small very basic restaurant also with a pool room and arcade games, a glass shop and an auto body shop. A wine store, a bookstore that also sold school supplies and a Chinese restaurant. A Hardware store would finalize the selection we had available to us. This was good. It appeared to be balanced enough. The bookstore and Chinese restaurant were the only Mozambicans in the mix but then a new cafe owned by a very nice gentleman from Cape Verde and another one in the opposite corner, complemented well; a new grocery store owned by a northern Portuguese who later sold it to a nice Afghani family. With new acquaintances and places to hang out and reminisce about our African experiences we felt more equipped to take our integration to the next step. One of the apartments above the strip mall had for a tenant the family of one of my good Mozambique friends. She was the first close connection I had in this corner of the world. Her brother, also a good friend and myself, shared some of the most common practices in the field of casual enjoyment, staples of the late decade of the 70s, before he became a respected judge. But now we were all sharing the same sentiment, teaching each other the different slangs that once displayed our differences turned now into an element of unity. In Africa without television broadcast, it was common for us all to play practical games at times. These were traditional children's games some originating in the sixteen and seventeen centuries, with the magic of bringing laughter to every participating player as well as the cheering squads, mainly composed by friends and families. In Africa all we needed was an acceptable number of players. Once we found we had enough, everyone was on board. In the summer since it started getting darker later, we used several times the parking lot of the strip mall for our field of play, and not surprising to us, some of the owners of the stores, regardless of their age came to join us. For us Africans there were no age limitations, and our screams of support and our cheers brought us back to a time when this was such a welcome activity in our gatherings. We found out after the second or third time we decided to play how different our mentalities were compared to the traditional Portuguese from Europe. The police were called on us and we were forced to stop and abandon this new found past time or be fined and even arrested for what they considered "disorderly conduct". As much as we tried to understand what could have possessed someone anonymously to call the cops on us it was hard to assimilate. We were really a different breed of people and it was starting to show. Even in the simple way we enjoy each other's company playing a simple brainless medieval game. I came to the understanding that it does not matter what age we are, we may stop being a child but never lose our childhood. Our childhood just gets placed inside a drawer kept in the farthest back area of our minds, like a special box or an old trunk with a lock where we keep our best memories, getting dust in our attics, until we accidentally come across it again while scavenging through the clutter. I learned now after all these years, and with the wisdom my age has flattered me with, that there are only three stages in a human being's life in which we are actually happy. Happy in the purest sense of the word. In our childhood where all innocence is obliged, when we truly fall in love and when for the first time we meet the eyes of our grandchildren. When you look into the eyes of someone you truly love or meet the eyes of your children's children the wrongs of the World suddenly vanish, a language is created with instant communication between souls, bigger than just joy, an exhilaration of happiness only partially visible from the outside. No language or science can explain the speed your entire being is moving hidden to the naked eye, sheltered from the evils we end up learning about, felt as if one has been hit by a thousand bolts of lightning that paralyze time and numb the senses. Those moments cannot be translated or explained with complex chemical reactions in the brain or by erudite thesis on emotions. Those moments transcend our understanding. They are not part of our human realm, they belong to the divine. Why would these neighbors rob us all of the innocence of our childhood again only for brief moments while playing a traditional game? What catastrophe happened in their lives that caused them to reject the opportunity, as Hemingway once said, of "mastering their adulthood by allowing their old age to acquire the courage to do what children do when they know nothing"? Had these complainers known that if given us a chance, they would also have the opportunity to get some joy out of a life under already very challenging circumstances?

30

Sisyphus is one of the most interesting characters in the Greek Mythology and of the ever chaotic and prodigal dysfunctionality of their family of gods. The son of the man that ruled the winds, this guy was smart and cunning to the point that he managed to cheat death not once but twice. First by brute force and the second time using diplomacy. In the realm of the humans this often is in our days how powers are taken down and replaced, but Sisyphus' clever trickery was somewhat original. The Greek mythology tells us that he was the first king of Corinth, and to his credit also the father of what we know now to be the Olympic Games, at the time called the Isthmian games because of taking place in the Isthmus of Corinth. After dying and descending into Hades, "the most cunning of men", as the Iliad puts it, managed to capture and chain Death, so that no other human being would have to face it ever again. Luckily for Death the god of war Ares found what had happened and freed him from the chains. The god of war needed Death free to roam at will and well in full function of his talents. Death needed to be alive and well. This of course was not good news for Sisyphus who could not escape the natural order of things as determined by the gods, ending up dying for the second time and descending again into the dark depths of Hades. Here is where he now displayed his special talents in the arts of diplomacy. Sisyphus had ordered his wife not to proceed upon his death with the normal rituals of the offerings and sacrifices due during traditional burial ceremonies. With his clever insight he realized that Persephone, Hades' wife, was extremely kind hearted and using the full power of his irresistible charm he pleaded with Persephone to get in Hades ear to allow him to go back, so he could make sure that all the rituals would be performed in order for everything to be according to the law. All would be made well again and he would then return. Needless to say, once he found himself back in the realm of the living he couldn't care less about his part of the bargain and simply did not go back. Hades, still traumatized by the experience of being chained, would not dare go near him, so it took the direct intervention of the god in charge Zeus, who became really irritated by Sisyphus' deception and audacity. To correct this defiance, as a punishment for all mankind to see that he had in his hands the designs of life and no other human would be encouraged to learn from Sisyphus cunning abilities, he condemned him to climb a mountain carrying a large stone only to get to the top where, before being able to topple it to the other side, watch it tumble over him and roll back to the depth of Hades, where he would have to start the climb all over again. Sisyphus had to repeat this ritual every day, over and over again for the rest of his existence.

I think that many if not most of the African returnees felt that their lives were Sisyphusian ones, condemned to no fault of their own, to be living in tedious, futile and hopeless labor, as in being caught in the fate wheel of the goddess Fortuna with no upside to it until their days on this earth were over, and they were called to enjoy eternal rest. Not my mother. She still scouted the horizon, eyes wide open, ears in full attention mode to capture every sound, mouth semi opened ready to bite, the heart beating in an accelerated but controlled pace. I believe now she never cared enough about the top of the mountain and what to do with the heavy boulder life had made her carry. Her focus was instead in every step she took, one steady step at a time. Life had shown her that as long as she had her cubs within reach, no rain or dry season would be a match for her tenacity and fortitude and that every step along the way was more important than what she would find at the next one or at the end of the journey. With her watching over us, with the backup of all the Saints she had come to know after finding comfort in their wisdom through a lot of prayer - she was constantly praying - and the prescriptions of some priests, my brother and I felt we could face anything. This lioness was a force to be reckoned with.

31

Almost two years had passed since I stepped inside that damn plane to cross over the African continent and I was feeling tired. Mentally exhausted, feeling like I was walking on this endless and empty road with no direction signs anywhere to be found. This was not an unexpected development, since my new found friends and I saw ourselves with nowhere to go. Thanks to our parents we were able to survive on very little. We didn't need much and our imaginations compensated for the rest. Portugal was going through a very deep economic crisis, with constant political fights and the government alternating from the Communists, to the Socialists and now with new intruders in the political fray, the Social Democrats. This was a welcome addition to the political spectrum. Social Democrats were more centrists, and even though they opened the door to movements leaning more to the Right, a lot of Portuguese citizens were not anymore willing to experience extremisms of any kind after fifty years of Fascist dictatorship. Some of the most revolutionary reforms in protection of the working class however took form in this still politically naive society. Portugal was proficuous in intellectuals, with everything gravitating around political ideologies and debates. This was however important in the maturity growth of these people and our own. Us Africans really had no idea what the Inter Sindical was for example. The most powerful Union in the world, with a clear Marxist Leninist line, managed in France to stay above the politics of the moments, while controlling the destiny of all political outcomes. Their representation of the labor class made it the most powerful and rich Union in the world. No enterprise however small or big, dared mess with this communist Union. Like no other I saw them effectively bring countries to a complete halt, regardless of the sector of the economy they wanted to impact. From nurses, to policemen and even judges, they had a particular technique to motivate workers to adhere to full strike mode, supported by their monetary infrastructure and putting the bosses against the wall. I never saw the Union lose a claim be it from salary to health benefits. We Africans were not yet familiarized with this reality. We had the experience of going from a dictatorship to a different kind of dictatorship. From Fascism to Communism, and even though once our perception started to adapt to a new reality and our minds ready to accept that, transition periods in these circumstances may have required an iron fist, we did not understand what it really meant to paralyze the dynamic of a society trying to move forward and prosper after over a half a century of oppression. During these troubled times, we realized that our experience, rich as it was, had no good use in this climate. It was a humbling experience to find out that we needed to bring Africa now to these shores and forget about adopting the Portuguese way of life if we wanted to survive.

32

In my new neighborhood there were three Victors. This was strange to me. I was used to being the only one within reach for most of my life. I was the youngest of the three, but I would have never imagined that one of these Victors would have an active role and impact my life forever. One was a simple honest man with a heart moved by the most acute sense of decency. He owned a small shop where he repaired and created glass windows, panes and all kinds of glass work. Mr. Victor number 1 had a faithful companion. A yellow short hair medium size dog with characteristics that could relate to about a half a dozen breeds, a mutt in the truest sense of the word. I can't remember the name of the dog but everywhere Victor went so did he, never on a leash but faithfully with his nose kept by his master's legs. This dog travelled on the passenger seat never in the back of the truck and Victor would only patronize places that would accept his faithful companion's admission, be it in a Tavern (Victor could not frequent fancy restaurants since dogs would not be allowed) or a pool hall where we often met for a good game of snooker or 8 ball. On a particular afternoon, while we were playing in the back room Victor's mutt for some inexplicable reason wandered away. I still see Victor fully concentrated on his stroke when an excruciating sound that sounded like a dog in pain came from the other side of the hall where the dining tables and the bar were. There was no need for further verification, Victor recognized that sound immediately, dropped the cue and ran to the next room only to find his dog limping and in pain. Victor did not ask any questions, and only a very momentary moment of reason prevented him from impaling the owner of the bar who had savagely hit the poor mutt in the back with a large stick trying to make it leave the room. For the longest time he had shown signs that even though he had allowed the pup's presence in the premises he was not a fan. The dog was friendly and comfortable. There was no one he was not familiar with, and if someone new would show up he had no reason to distrust them. It liked humans. I ran after Victor to make sure he did not act in haste and risked getting arrested. After all he was one of us. All I remember was Victor behind the counter, his right hand around the throat of the owner who was by the way much bigger than him, and with a voice that sounded like the anchor from "The voice of the Jungle", his teeth clenched to concentrate all his strength on the fingers holding the owners neck saying, "If you are not man enough to face up to men, do not take it up on the dog". This was the last time we ever played in that place we had loved and enjoyed for so long ever again. We all left without another word. It hurt and saddened us but our loyalty to our friends was worth a lot more than our mundane desires. Victor had a heart like few. He was fueled by basic decency.

33

Steve was almost thirty years old, had a very thick moustache that one only sees in some characters of movies portraying the fashion concepts from the early beginnings of the nineteenth century. Also a returnee from Angola, I rarely spoke with him and never saw him with a partner, a companion or a family member. He did not appear to have many friends either, and often I saw Steve at the place we used to patronize, always eager to find somebody with whom to strike a conversation no matter what about. He did not seem unhappy at all, but lonely at least, no doubt. His way of presenting himself and how he dressed, gave us an indication that he was the only one caring for himself. We used to say "hi" every time we met in the same place, some very basic courtesies and join my crew to do whatever we struck our fancy at the moment and many times, Steve would just very quietly insinuate himself towards us. We always had our arms open to him, We in a way felt sorry for the man but he was not easy to talk to and we sensed we had very little in common aside from these occasions to get together either at a game of pool or pinball. Then it so happened that I had beat everybody to the place that afternoon when Steve was the only recognizable face sitting at the counter having lunch, which did not give me the luxury of multiple choice so I sat by his side. To make this moment more comfortable I had asked for an espresso and joined in the habitual exercise of finding something to talk about. I can't remember how or why, he made me aware that he was looking for a helper for a job he had just undertaken, that included a project from a local theater group. The job was to build a scenery for a play or a show of some kind coming to town, as he put it. Then without firing a warning shot he asked me if I was interested in making a few bucks on the side. Well, at the moment I had nothing better to do so I said "sure", how much does it pay? Initially he hesitated but he looked somewhat in a hurry to get somebody which led me to believe he wasn't comfortable at all with the kind of work he was supposed to perform, and when he suggested that we became partners, it also told me he had no idea how to perform it. I mean, how did he know if I would be able to help him or get it done successfully? Or was he looking for someone to ease the blow when he crashed and burned at some point in time after the truth revealed he had swallowed more than he could chew? I thought "partners? Sounds cool" and we shook hands. The next morning we both walked inside the warehouse store in the middle of the street to talk to the owner about what we needed.

34

Victor number 2 lived in the building right across the street from mine, a couple of floors below. He owned a warehouse store and had a daughter who studied classical piano. Every day we could hear her repeat the same movements for hours. She was persistent, disciplined and I am sure she became an excellent player or at least a good piano teacher. Don't think she made it in the artistic world. Maybe some good orchestra. Victor was a smart man, more polished and with a much better vocabulary than our friend Victor number 1 with his dog. He also had a good sense of what it meant to be involved in some kind of community involvement. He had this keen sense of community activism that could expand his customer base, and concerning this investment in particular he did not look to be very frugal. In the end like most of us he was a good family man, able to shield his family for the most part from the neighborhood unknowns, and totally focused in providing a good living to those who depended on him, a prosperous business and a good education for his daughter. Victor was directly involved in a small community guild that provided a simple lodge very much like a veterans hall to locals, who needed a place to have special events or just go to a bar and have a couple of cheap drinks. Among some of the activities the guild availed to the community was a small amateur theater troupe - there was a reasonable size stage in the main hall - run by a man who had all his family involved in this venture. I went to meet this man and whomever else was involved. Along with Steve and Victor that same evening of the day I walked inside his store to talk about supplies. His answer at the time was "Let's meet this evening at the guild, and you will be able to learn what it is we have in mind and what is needed". So we did.

35

More times than I can count I had passed in front of this collectivity without even noticing it. The sign on the wall by the door was old and small and unless you were one of the old school inhabitants in the historic part of this lovely village there was no way of knowing. The historic section of the village was small, a half a dozen small cobblestone roads and a main artery which would snake down towards the Palace of the Marquis. Coming down the local square was dominated by an old church in honor of Our Lady of the Purification which started being built in 1702. This part of the village was situated between two major hills, one going up towards where we lived and the other going towards the railway station.

Steve and I knocked at the door at about 7:30 that evening. An old and tired man who did not know how to smile opened the door and let us in. It was dark, and even in the main hall where the stage was located the lights were dim, only contrasting with the activity on the stage fully lit, where a couple of adults and mostly teenagers around my age were talking loudly and keeping themselves with "things". Victor had been there with the leader of this group waiting for us. Never did I know or could have imagined that this man would become indelibly etched in my life forever. His name was Al, and he was a very affable late 40's man, very cordial with a warm smile and a frank friendly tingle in his eye. I sensed he was a people's person. Just one of those people that help brighten this world filled with misery and distrust. One of those souls put on this earth to help us keep our balances and sanity. We all shook hands and Victor took the lead. He was older than Al and a respected guy from what I detected. I figured he had the money needed for this project and the necessary connections, so he was worthy of some deference. Steve assumed of course the lead role on our side, smiling a lot, not asking any questions and allowing his head almost robotly to nod "yes, amen" at will, giving me heartburn and Victor and Al the impression that this was not a problem, and practically a done deal the moment it had been thought of. Al's oldest daughter, one of six, five girls and one boy the second oldest, joined the conversation to be introduced to us at her father's request. I realized she must have been the lead person of the crew when it came to the players part, and maybe just because she was her father's apple of his eyes. I did my part, knew no one and was not really interested in staying much longer. It struck me as odd that there was no talk whatsoever about how much we would charge for the work that up to that point none of us knew what it entailed. We said our goodbyes and left. Steve was enthusiastic about this, I not so much since besides meeting some interesting people I had still no perception if anything had changed since before we walked in to meet them. I could not ever have perceived this moment to be the one that would transform my life forever.

36

It took me the next day to get to the bottom of what it was we really needed to be doing, and how serious this all project was. I summoned Steve to the restaurant and asked him to walk with me to Victor's store. I had found out that he was donating to the show the troupe was preparing, all the supplies needed for building the scenario. "So tell me again a bit more in detail what we are supposed to do here" I told Victor with much needed assertion, "what is the idea?" I asked. He was a bit taken back by my lack of knowledge and very politely asked Steve if he had filled me in, he had not I believe, mainly because of total ignorance regarding how to do the work. Nevertheless Victor told me that the troupe had decided to organize their own version of a very popular TV contest show in our community, dedicated to young children and by young children with prizes donated by the local store owners and different organizations with their residence in the township. And since the TV show's main character was a cow, here it would be a duck. "Cute" I thought. So I was finally filled in the details.

There were different themes, with questions and variety acts, judged by a panel of judges which would by the process of elimination after a few weeks elect a winner. I got the info and went back to the cafe for an espresso and a talk with Steve who was starting to irritate me a bit more with his robotic nod of "no problem". At this point I was getting more comfortable with him and besides I could very well use the money. When we sat down and I asked him if he had any idea how to go about this, he blabbered a lot of nonsense and to my dismay he had no idea of even how to dress the background or the scenario. All he had was a basic knowledge of how to nail together a few pieces of wood to build a hopefully solid structured frame. But…..what about the scenario? It dawned on me right there and then, that my primitive talent in drawing had to step up to the plate or this would be humiliating, never mind ruining a complete project idealized by so many important people not to mention a breach of contract and false representation. My "finger in the face" and "fatherly talk about Isabel" cousin, who in my eyes was a real artist, encouraged me constantly to keep drawing since I was a little boy and I used to spend a lot of time watching him draw after my father died. He convinced me that I also had a talent worthy of being explored and practiced drawing a lot. That was what saved our honor. I would not settle for less especially because of how close our common geographies we were.

37

I drew some "sketches" in A4 papers and brought them in person to the troupe leader for approval. Steve came along of course. Al had his oldest daughter and son with him. I could see how close they were since he really valued their opinions and not only that, he was constantly encouraging their input. They were beautiful, these girls. And fully involved. I could see how seriously they took their roles in this troupe. There were a couple of adults also who ran the backstage including an electrician and a jack of all trades who rented a room in Al's house. The only son of this family was an athletic handsome soccer player at the local team, and to my surprise Al also ran a small soccer academy for kids starting to kick a ball more officially in the town. How and where did this man find the time to do all this and still have a regular job? As I started to work on the panels to dress the stage, I became better acquainted with everybody and felt particularly welcome within the family. Night after night we would go to the upper room at the guild to work, and the fact that I was extra careful with the details in the panels put us significantly behind our schedules. This was a problem. I wished then and there that I had been more secure about my ability to draw, and Steve of course was not much of an artist, so it was not surprising to me that in light of this about to be classified as a major setback, the three older siblings Tina, Mario and Leonor came to help. We all became very close friends. Leonor was the youngest of the three and she had a discreet feistiness that I could sense, with very concealed lewd looks and I was enjoying this very much almost making me lose my focus, but there was someone else in the room that I was forcefully trying to avoid. This long hair blonde and hazel eyed girl had me lose my sleep. She had a perfect body and an unassumed simplicity, an innocent joy in being, adorned with a smile so radiant that fed me plenty in my fantasies. No way in hell I would have a chance here. This was a minefield and I would not allow myself to be humiliated by stepping on one. Nah! The odds were much better with her beautiful sister with dark hair and chocolate brown eyes. We spent hours drawing and painting as the deadline was mercilessly approaching, and one night while walking home with Steve - we walked everywhere fearlessly at any time day or night in that coastal village - in his lack of infinite wisdom he tells me that he is going to court Tina, the blonde as he put it, and ask her to be his girlfriend. I did not believe he was her type, but the audacity of even just having the thought made me angry, and using his preferred expression I nodded and said "yes, you should!" He then suggested that I should try to get her sister. This was obviously not well planned in his mind, and I felt even a bit insulted with the thought that I could and should try to get my hands on a less valuable prize. This was not the case at all, Leonor had that special lure of the European Latina that the world is incapable of not noticing, but there was no way I would let Steve stain with his touch this newly found Aphrodite that had fallen in my universe. I was irritated but smiled back at Steve wishing in the back of my mind that he would try if he dared. I was confident but, since beauty as the saying goes, was in the eyes of the beholder, one never knows. Had she given him a sign, an inkling of any sort that made him think this was possible? I could not sleep that night very peacefully, but had no strategy, and my lack of confidence was not helping. I decided to change my strategy from trying to come up with a way to be noticed by her, to one to make sure Steve would not have a bite at that apple. The thought that she was not a fan of moustaches comforted me. I knew no one in her family, of those I had met, who had one. This was definitely not her type. With this in mind I felt better and was finally able to close my eyes and sleep.

38

The next day I could hardly disguise my anxiety. I could not wait for the evening to go back to work on the panels. Nothing I did until then registered in my memory that day. My body was a mechanical piece in auto pilot, my mind remained somewhere else until the time came to go to work. I did not wait for Steve who was usually a bit delayed for no apparent or even acceptable reason, so I proposed that we meet at guild. I could not believe my eyes when I saw him walking in with his moustache shaved off. What was this after all, could I have been wrong in my assumptions and would it be possible that such a beautiful girl had such horrible taste? I was unhappy, until I decided that with or without a moustache Steve was still Steve. As we worked into the night, these three siblings, especially Tina showed me something I didn't know I had. A sense of humor. I had forgotten since being ripped from my roots only a couple of years ago, how funny I could be at times. I had lost all interest in even being a pleasant company. Until this night my thoughts were still deep far in a corner of south east Africa, even though I had a new chance at friends, new beaches and places to find. All I remember is them laughing out loud at what I cannot remember I was doing or saying. I loved making this girl laugh, but mostly I loved her laughter, her perfect snow white teeth and bright eyes just lighting up the room. Nothing else mattered, yet again, this seemed too much out of my league. The job had been completed, the show was a success, and to my surprise Al asked me to join the troupe. I was happy designing the scenery but he wanted me to be on stage, which I was very uncomfortable with. This only gave me the opportunity to be closer to her for longer periods of time. This was a dynamic group, with an inexhaustible fountain of love to share. Hesitantly I accepted the challenge and as expected was not good at it at all, but I started feeling like I had found what I felt long lost. A new family. Not just relatives but a family who would share mealtimes together with a lot to talk about. Al and his unemployed wife, six children to look after and an under paying job, never showed me any disappointment for having to put an extra plate at the table in spite of their struggle, and I started abusing my welcome. I started going to their house at dinner time a lot. I was happy, and not ready to see Tina, one day walking in with a new boyfriend, and if it happened to be Steve, this would be Gisela all over again, but until that moment had come to pass, I stood steadfastly enjoying every trip to a stage somewhere in the region to perform for locals at other small villages. It was in one of these tours in November that when leaving the stage and going behind the scenes to change my custom, Arthur who lived at the house, called me aside and whispered "you know that bracelet Tina is wearing? The silver one? She had your name engraved in it!" I thought he was joking, played the macho card and acted uninterested, but after we were done and everybody went home, I was trying to make sense of all of it. Could it really be? I was going to tell Steve, but then the devil sitting on top of my shoulder suggested that I showed him instead. On Friday nights it was normal for us to hangout for longer and unbeknownst to me Arthur had organized for all of us just to go stay at the beach for a couple of hours. We were a large group, boys and girls from the troupe and Arthur. I think they planned it carefully, so when we got to the beach Tina and myself sat on a large rock watching the waves dance in the moonlight, and instead of everybody staying together as usual, they all moved away leaving us both alone. She was wearing a large green winter coat with a hood, and blue jeans. I did not say much and neither did she. We practically stayed there staring at the ocean, smoking a cigarette, or two. The time came for us to walk home, and again after the first steps we both stayed behind the very vociferous happy crew ahead of us. I looked at her face and she was not happy. Really I had put her in a bad mood. She probably felt that this was a waste of time or I did not care, but in reality I was trying to push the boundaries, almost forcing her to make the first move. She was too proud for that though. As we came into the gardens that accessed her house and everybody was saying their goodbyes, I reached to her and we kissed. I don't know for how long we kissed. But I did not want to leave her lips. It took the group a third or fourth call for me to let her go. One thing was for sure. I knew deep in my heart that my life had forever changed. This was the first day of our lives together.

39

Steve had now left the group understandingly, since at his age the priority was to find a job and build a life. I did not get a congratulatory tap on the shoulder or a hand shake but he was gracious enough to wish me a very happy life with Tina. We dated for almost three years and I discovered Lisbon with her. After that first kiss she had to go away on a family function leaving me in a desert thirsty and with no water in sight, but coming Monday I went to pick her up after work. I figured this would make our relationship more official. She was a clerk at the office of a local factory which employed close to sixty people.

This was the same company her father worked for, just in a different location. Her place of employment was in a zone called Alcantara, about 2 miles from downtown Lisbon. This was a prank done by the Universe since Alcantara is exactly the town I had been born in, and knew nothing about. An industrialized part of Lisbon with lots of trolley traffic and cobblestone sidewalks. Her office was on the top of three very large stone flights of steps and I waited at the bottom for her to come down. Did not take long for this vision from my invented paradise to come down, wearing a plaid shirt and tight burgundy corduroy pants. Her long blond hair waving at every step she took down those stairs and a smile that the sun used as a mirror to check itself out before going to work. I could not take my eyes off her, not wanting to lose her sight in case this was not real, but she kept coming down steadily, put her arms around my waist and said "hi". The kiss she gave me injected my lips with a flavor that remains fresh until today. She was the oldest of the family and of course our relationship became the talk and the curiosity of grandparents, cousins and friends. She was a prize indeed, and because of who she was very few doors remained unopened. The Portuguese in general have no defense mechanism against beautiful women. We walked the streets of Lisbon often, and traveled to different places, went to see the Pope when he visited Portugal, as the good Old Catholic tradition recommended. To have this kind of connection with a true family gave me some sustenance. I had found the love of my life and inherited a family.

40

My mother had been back for a while at home now and I took Tina to meet her. This was an important step mostly for me, and for the first time I felt no need to gain the lioness's approval. I could see in my mother's eyes when she looked at me that she understood where my heart was. I think she started to face the inevitable cycle of her youngest cub leaving the pride. She wanted to go back to Coimbra to visit and Tina to come with us to meet the entire family on our side there. She knew, my mother that is. This was not customary unless you were engaged or married. We got lost in the streets of old medieval Coimbra, still today one of our favorite cities in Portugal, lost in the traditions, lost in the array of pastries and baked goods it had to offer. We allowed ourselves to get lost in the "garden of the sirens" and in the "estate of tiers", where one of the most beautiful and tragic love stories happened during the Portuguese monarchy of the XIV century. My uncles and aunts loved Tina so much that they offered to organize everything to make it possible for us to move to Coimbra. We were grateful but I knew that the bond left behind in Oeiras was too great and I was okay with it. Life moved along. Since I had been born in Portugal I was drafted to the army. There was in my mind absolutely no logic in this, the war had been over now, and I could not see any justification, but had no choice. With the possibility of deploying overseas since Portugal was an active member of NATO now that Africa was no longer monopolizing the Portuguese resources, out on a whim we decided to get married. I did not get on my knees, and did not know how to ask her father for his daughter's hand in marriage, this was to us both a logical materialization of part of our destiny. No mystery at all. To this day, in the deepest part of my heart I feel a certain remorse for not doing it the proper way for this man, my future father-in-law who respected and accepted me as one of his children, but this was aggravated by the fact that we decided to marry while I was still in the service. Obviously the first thought that came to her father's mind when I "communicated" to him that "we were going to get married", his first instinct was to turn to his daughter and ask if she was pregnant. He knew she would never lie to him. She wasn't, so immediately with the love and compassion this many had plenty of, he lectured me to make sure I understood how disappointed he was, however he looked at his daughter's eyes and saw a sadness that he could not bear. She wanted his approval, to see him happy with our decision regardless of the habitual courtesies, we were in love and were going nowhere. Resigned to this new reality, he hugged her and shook my hand. I made a decision that day to do whatever I could in my power to make sure I would not disappoint him. Eight months later we got married in the large Church of the Village Square and everybody from North to South that was family along with friends came to the wedding. As I was there the thought did not cross my mind, but sometime later I wondered about the joy my African buddies must have felt if they were here.

41

Africa kept me at bay. The park in front of our house in LM had been given the name of a first lady of the Republic in the decade of the fifties. To my surprise the park still holds her name. We had been friends with one of her daughters, and her four sons were close friends of mine. I never saw either of them again and thought about them often. It was totally unexpected when I came to find out that our neighbor in the next door apartment was their cousin. Rachel was older and single, living with her mother, Very quiet and extremely discreet both of them, used from time to time to come and visit us, talking in mysterious whispers with my mother which always caught my curiosity but I had other things to think about. Sporadically in the quietness of the night she used to get the visit of a large African man, always well dressed in what looked like a designer suit, who would stay for a couple of hours and leave afterwards. My mother knew this man. He was a politician getting his education in Europe we presumed, however a few months later after quite a few of his visits Rachel opened the book. He was in clandestinely forming a new Party to challenge the one presently in power, the Frelimo, trying to attract support from different sources in case he would have to engage in military conflict. Once I found this out the only thought coming to my mind was that if this movement succeeded in generating a new war, then all my hope for my friends left behind would vanish. There was indeed the insurgency of a new war, but the capital was spared the bloodshed. Years later already in this century this gentleman did become president. He was the brother of the officer that implored aboard the liner that would bring my mother to Europe, for her to stay. Sometimes it felt Africa never left.

42

Exactly one year and one day later after we got married our first daughter was born. This was the most anticipated news in the family since according to the natural order of things we should have children first. We were older and got married first. The Portuguese elders, especially the women, have this invisible calendar ingrained in their minds that determines when the continuance of the family lineage needs to take place. We had moved into my own apartment with my mother. Portugal was in a deep economic crisis, still under political turmoil and lack of jobs. The job market was a savage one.

In Europe to have a degree from any superior academic institute grants the grad a special statute in society. The social classes were well defined. A lawyer would practice law, a doctor would practice medicine, an engineer or an architect would work in their respective fields. This dividing line that establish the differences among the classes became blurred with the loss of the African colonies, and now the country had lost its ability to drain the work force to different sectors, the result was that a lawyer or a historian or an engineer for instance would apply to any job opening and with that, there were a lot of grads performing work they would have despised otherwise. This made the competitiveness of the market unbearable and jobs kept getting lost at the pace that different companies were closing their doors. I had been lucky. I was first employed by the branch of Rank Xerox to sell copy machines, and then by an insurance company as a complaint clerk. Insurance and banking jobs were highly prized at the time, and without the proper connections it would be practically impossible to get one. I had gotten in, and with an excellent job performance started quickly gaining ground, but not without some unfriendly stares from those who were starting to feel threatened by the new intern. During those days, for the major part everybody got their feet in these multinationals as interns, and upon proving themselves they would become what was then known as effective employees. I had no fear and my brother Paulo had serious connections in the industry, nothing would happen to me for sure. In my naiveté I thought that since this was a Swiss outfit, the afflictions of their Portuguese cohorts would not affect us. We were walking on solid ground, our daughter was close to becoming five years old, loved by all as the legitimate heiress to the throne of the family, and even in the middle of the crisis we had no worries. For the first time in a long time, I started getting the feeling that this could be the ground where I could finally rest upon and develop new roots. I had felt like a man without a homeland for so long. Now I believed the time had come. I had found new fertile soil and this was finally home. Until exactly with one week to go into my change of status at work I received notice that my position would not be renewed. I was going to be terminated exactly 24 hours before my three years of work were completed to prevent the company from hiring me effectively. This was a common tactic known to everybody, just the way the game was played but for some reason I thought that being benched would be the worst that could happen to me, never in my worst case scenario I thought I would be ejected from the team. The level of injustice that I felt was easy to describe in some very explicit words and I tried to have my immediate supervisor learn what they were.

43

I kept reflecting about the fact that I had been through what was enough to give me the necessary strength to resist the political landscape and sooner or later come on to the other side. I was tired of changing the North in my compass. I came to know this city, this country. I came to enjoy heavy dinners at 11:00 pm while listening to the Fado in smoke filled dim lighted houses. I came to appreciate the aromas of the hundreds of pastry shops with baked goods displayed in their counties resembling Christmas lights. I loved going out to the beach sometimes as early as February and as late as November, the get together with friends and family and really have subjects to talk about. To go and see the original lampposts from even before the 1775 earthquake and how some houses still had the original door knobs, I loved crossing paths with centuries of history at every corner, yes this was home and it was time to stop feeling like an endless chase of the wind. Everything is temporary, this too shall pass, I was thinking in an attempt to forbid myself from succumbing to doubt. Invaded by mixed feelings I sat down in the living room across from my mother. I could see in her the signs of a lioness not getting any younger, some grey hairs denouncing the hidden scars of a life spent fighting and in her countenance, signs of worry. She worried, prayed and hoped. Worried, prayed and hoped, that her cubs would find a companion, a partner that would protect them when her body and mind could not cover the savannah as fast as she used to, and her strike in the face of danger would not be as powerful. What would happen to them, did she teach them well how to fend for themselves? The answer to her anguish came within minutes with a phone call. I was on my way back from the kitchen when Tina answered the phone, and I could see standing under the kitchen entrance, that she was serious almost solemnly for a while without saying much besides some yeses and hums. From her greeting I knew this was my oldest brother. Our phone was located on top of a camphor chest facing another one made of ebony encrusted with mother pearl motifs. Maybe the only large pieces of furniture my mother managed to bring over from Africa. She hung up the phone, and this was the moment that my mother's agony could finally be unfelt to allow her to tilt her head back and give her mind the peace she had been yearning for. This cub of hers had found the right companion, the partner she was hoping and praying for, a younger lioness with plenty of muscle in her spirit. Tina approached me with that same smile that from the first day still imprisons my senses, placed her arms around my neck and with a sweet whisper told me "Baby, we are going to America!"

MORE ABOUT THE BOOK

The conflicts we struggle with every day are (for the most part) what societies all around the world have mostly in common. This is a story about the experience of growing up in an area of conflict, contrasting with a totally different reality, one where the birth of new and revolutionary social rules were a source of turmoil; colored by the influence of different cultures, behaviors, and environments. The endless search for answers permanently presents the author with new questions. Questions which make him a stoic proponent of a better society where justice and equality are made available to everyone regardless of the color of their skin, their origin, or gender. In today's digital world where borders are more and more dissipated by the power of digital media in small hand held devices, the challenges of nations regardless of where they sit in the hierarchy of advanced civilizations become more apparent, there are no perfect hidden Edens on earth. There is only an uncomfortable commonality that makes us as the human race more alike regardless of our geographies.

MORE ABOUT THE AUTHOR

Victor Dias DeSousa has been a resident of the great State of New Jersey for over three decades, but still considers himself a Global resident. He has experienced life on three different continents and enjoyed the waters of two different oceans during two of the most defining decades of the 19th century. His daughters and grandsons have grown up with stories of remote tribes, warm salty lagoons, espresso in Lisbon, soccer clubs, motorcycles, and even the African lions being told to them from across the living room couch and dinner table. The realization that regardless of the diversity of our geographies we all as mankind pursue the same dreams and enjoy the same aspirations in life is what inspired Victor Dias DeSousa to finally share a taste of these stories with the world. There are no heroes or villains. Just people and experiences he met along the journey. Sharing these stories the author wants to preserve the fantasies in the imagination of those who dream of distant lands, strange rituals and cultures, and hopes to stimulate the desire of leaving the comfort of our own abodes and brave new worlds.

Made in the USA
Middletown, DE
15 November 2020